Competition Law, Regulation, and Digital Platforms

This book confronts and analyses how competition law in its present form is unable to deal with the new advances in digital technology that have made tech giants not subject to national jurisdictions as they straddle the world, with a particular focus on Japan, China, UK, EU, and USA.

Demonstrating how the gatekeeping role of digital platforms has broken through the boundaries of national regulation, this book highlights examples where companies have broken and infringed antitrust law with impunity, pursuing self-preferencing and unfair competition practices solely for their own profitability. It also identifies how tech giants can open their digital platforms for fair use by consumers, small and medium enterprises (SMEs), and creators, while still allowing tech giants to maintain their important role as gatekeepers of digital security that protects users from cyberattacks. This is followed by an examination of the similarities between tech giants and big pharma within the competition law and intellectual property context, revealing how tech giants are beginning to target the healthcare sector.

Exploring how intellectual property rights are interwoven through new modernising regulations to curtail the dominance of Big Tech on digital platforms, this book will appeal to students, scholars, and practitioners of Business Ethics, Intellectual Property, Law, and Regulation.

Ruth Taplin (PhD London School of Economics and Political Science [LSE] and Graduate Diploma in Law) is Director of the Centre for Japanese and East Asian Studies, London, Editor/Founder of the *Interdisciplinary Journal of Economics and Business Law* (IJEBL). Professor Taplin is the author/editor of 28 books and over 200 articles. Early on in her career she was chosen as a future leader in the Japanese field for the UK.

Kazuhiko Fuchikawa is an Associate Professor of Competition Law at Keio University, Japan. Professor Fuchikawa is a winner of the Masatoshi Yokota Memorial Award (New Face Award of the Japan Association of Economic Law), 2015.

Routledge Studies in the Growth Economies of Asia

153 The Political Economy of Redistribution in Indonesia
Political Patronage and Favoritism in Intergovernmental Fiscal Transfer Allocations
Gerrit J. Gonschorek

154 Ethnicity and Development
Addressing the Gaps in New Institutional Economics
Shahrukh Rafi Khan

155 India's Economic Corridor Initiatives
INSTC and Chabahar Port
Kashif Hasan Khan

156 East Asian Ethical Life and Socio-economic Transformation in the Twenty-First Century
The Ethical Sources of the Entrepreneurial Renewal of Companies and Communities
Edited by Carsten Herrmann-Pillath and Qian Zhao

157 Post-Pandemic Economic and Social Development
Recovery, Challenges, and Policy in Malaysia
Edited by Muzalwana Abdul Talib, Ahmad Farid Osman, and Elya Nabila Abdul Bahri

158 Skills Formation for Economic Growth
The Case of Hong Kong
David Lim

159 Competition Law, Regulation and Digital Platforms
Japan, China, UK, EU and USA
Edited by Ruth Taplin and Kazuhiko Fuchikawa

Competition Law, Regulation, and Digital Platforms

Japan, China, UK, EU, and USA

Edited by Ruth Taplin and Kazuhiko Fuchikawa

Routledge
Taylor & Francis Group
LONDON AND NEW YORK

First published 2025
by Routledge
4 Park Square, Milton Park, Abingdon, Oxon OX14 4RN

and by Routledge
605 Third Avenue, New York, NY 10158

Routledge is an imprint of the Taylor & Francis Group, an informa business

British Library Cataloguing-in-Publication Data
A catalogue record for this book is available from the British Library

ISBN: 978-1-032-78854-8 (hbk)
ISBN: 978-1-032-78857-9 (pbk)
ISBN: 978-1-003-48954-2 (ebk)

DOI: 10.4324/9781003489542

Typeset in Times New Roman
by KnowledgeWorks Global Ltd.

Contents

Tables

Preface

Competition Law is currently seen as a vehicle for reducing consumer inequality and poverty, a role not previously contemplated. The EU/UK is leading such legislation with Japan not far behind, and USA making important regulatory contributions. Very little is known and has been written about this topic in the English language in relation to Japan. My distinguished colleagues whom I met with in Japan are the top experts in Competition Law who have agreed to contribute to this edited volume and write well in English. This book, therefore, makes a unique contribution to the current literature.

The most burning issue that this book will confront and analyse is that Competition Law in its present form is unable to deal with the new advances in digital technology that have made private sector behemoths, commonly known as tech giants, not subject to national jurisdictions as they straddle the world. Therefore, the gatekeeping role of digital platforms has broken through the boundaries of national regulation and pushed its ability to break antitrust law with impunity, pursuing unfair practice to its own advantage. How the tech giants use their digital platforms to their own unfair advantage vis-à-vis the regulators, nation states, consumers, and SME companies is analysed in this book. How regulators, nation states, consumers, and companies deal with the need to expand Competition Laws to include the new threats to unfair practices are assessed in Japan, China, UK, EU, and USA. Each of these regions of the world has unique contributions and challenges in modernising their Competition Laws to deal with such unprecedented dominance of digital platforms by the tech giants. Japan is especially caught in the middle of these challenges and in relation to the other geopolitical regions, while in Europe, Brexit has caused the UK to find solutions independent of the EU.

The other crucial issue is how tech giants can open their digital platforms for fair use that benefits consumers, SMEs, and creators while allowing tech giants to maintain their important role as gatekeepers of digital security that protects users from cyberattacks. This burning issue which poses a conundrum is yet to be solved and we explore possible solutions.

Additionally, Big Pharma also requires modernising within the Competition Law and Intellectual Property contexts as tech giants are beginning to target the healthcare sector. Intellectual Property Rights is interwoven through all the new regulation to curtail the dominance of Big Tech on digital platforms and either be part of unfair competition and attempts to combat it. Within this context there are implications for cyber risk.

Acknowledgements

Great thanks are due to the Great Britain Sasakawa Foundation grant support which made the lead Editor Ruth Taplin's visit to Japan in 2023 a reality to meet the excellent contributors to this book. Thanks are also due to Professor Masako Wakui, a Competition Law expert from Kyoto University, who hosted me at her seminar with her Graduate students.

Many thanks are also given to Professor Bartlomeij Nowak, Dean of the Law Department, Kozminski University, Poland, for hosting my lecture on 29 March 2023 at his Law Department which was the start of this book project.

We are indebted to the late Professor Valentine Korah formerly of University College London (UCL) who made an incalculable contribution to Competition Law as a discipline.

Abbreviations

ACM	Autoriteit Consument & Markt
AFA	Anti-fragmentation Agreements
AFS	AdSense for Search
AI	Artificial Intelligence
AWS	Amazon Web Services
B2B	business-to-business
BAT	Baidu, Alibaba, and Tencent
CBDC	Central Bank Digital Currency
CMA	Competition and Markets Authority
CSPs	cloud service providers
DA	Data Act
DMA	Digital Market Act
DOJ	Department of Justice
DPS	data processing services
DSA	Digital Services Act
EC	European Commission
ECJ	European Court of Justice
ESG	environmental, social, and governance
EU	European Union
FDA	Federal Drug Administration
fintech	financial technology
GAFA	Google, Amazon, Facebook, and Apple
GC	General Court
GDP	gross domestic product
GSA	Google Services Agreements
IaaS	infrastructure as a service
IJEBL	*Interdisciplinary Journal of Economics and Business Law*
IPR	Intellectual Property Rights
IT	information technology
JFTC	Japan Fair Trade Commission
KFTC	Korean Federal Trade Commission
LSE	London School of Economics and Political Science
M&A	mergers and acquisitions

METI	Japanese Ministry of Economy, Trade and Industry
MIC	Ministry of Internal Affairs and Communications of Japan
OFCOM	Office of Communications
Open AI	ChatGPT
OS	operating system
PaaS	platform as a service
QR	Quick Response code
R&D	research and development
SaaS	software as a service
SAMB	State Anti-Monopoly Bureau
SAMR	State Administration for Market Regulation
SCDMP	Japan Society of Community Disaster Management Plan
SMEs	small and medium sized enterprises
SNS	simple notification services
SSNIP	small but significant and non-transitory increase in price
TFEU	Treaty on the Functioning of the European Union
UCL	University College London
USFTC	US Federal Trade Commission
USPTO	United States Patent and Trademark Office
UTP	unshielded twisted pair
VIE	variable interest entities

Contributors

Kazuhiko FUCHIKAWA is an Associate Professor of Competition Law at Keio University (2024-present). He received a PhD in Law from Keio University in 2014. He was a Research Associate at Keio University (2012–2013); Assistant Professor (2013–2015) and Associate Professor (2015–2020) at Yamaguchi University; and Associate Professor at Osaka City University (2020–2022) and Osaka Metropolitan University (2023).

His principal writings include 'Comparative Analysis of the Japanese Subcontract Act and the Regulations on Unfair Trade Practices in the EU: Focus on the Grocery Industry' in Fabiana Di Porto, Rupprecht Podszun (eds.), *Abusive Practices in Competition Law* (Edward Elgar Publishing, 2018): 405–424; 'Regulations of Digital Platform Markets under the Japanese Antimonopoly Act: Does the Regulation of Unfair Trade Practices Solve the Gordian Knot of Digital Markets?' (2020) *The Antitrust Bulletin,* 65, 102–119.

Professor Fuchikawa is the winner of the Masatoshi Yokota Memorial Award (New Face Award of the Japan Association of Economic Law), 2015.

Shuya HAYASHI is a Professor of Law at Nagoya University Graduate School of Law. Professor Hayashi's main research area is Competition Law and Telecommunications/Broadcasting Law. He is a director of the Japan Society of Info-Communication Research, and a director of the Japan Society of Economic Law, the Japan Society of International Economic Law, and the Japan Society of Community Disaster Management Plan (SCDMP). He is also an advisory board member of the American Antitrust Institute.

Professor Hayashi is also actively engaged in making policy recommendations and deliberations in the area of competition and telecommunication/ law and policy. For example, he is a Commissioner of the Radio Regulatory Council, and Deputy Chair of the Telecommunications Market Review Board, Ministry of Internal Affairs and Communications of Japan (MIC). He is also a member of the Science Council of Japan.

Professor Hayashi is a winner of the DOCOMO Mobile Science Award (in the category of Social Science), Mobile Communication Fund 2020. He is also a winner of KDDI Research, Inc. NEXTCOM Best Paper Award 2021, and 2017 Best Paper Award of SCDMP.

Kentaro HIRAYAMA qualified as a lawyer in Japan in 2002, and has since built a distinguished 21-year career specialising in antitrust and competition law. From 2007 to 2010, he served as an investigator at Japan's Fair Trade Commission (JFTC), the sole regulator of competition law in the country. In addition to his legal practice, Dr Hirayama is actively involved in studying and teaching Competition Law. He held a position as an Associate Professor at Kyushu National University from 2018 to 2022, and then transitioned to the Institute of Business Science at Tsukuba National University.

Xiaofei LU received her PhD from Hitotsubashi University of Law and currently serves as an Associate Professor at the Graduate School of Business Administration, SBI Graduate University, in Tokyo. Dr Lu obtained her law degree from Shandong University in China and moved to Japan in 2005, where she completed her LLM and PhD studies at Hitotsubashi University. Before her current position, she worked as a specially appointed lecturer at Hitotsubashi University for two years in addition to serving as a visiting scholar at Taiwan University in Taiwan.

Specialising in company law, Dr Lu's research primarily focuses on the protection of shareholder rights and the regulation of corporate groups. She has authored numerous articles and presented at various conferences on topics related to safeguarding shareholder rights within parent-subsidiary companies. Additionally, Dr Lu actively delivers lectures at institutions such as Hitotsubashi University and other universities. She also provides legal consultancy services mainly in relation to company law as a practising Chinese lawyer in Japan.

Naoko MARIYAMA is Professor at Undergraduate School of Law, Tokai University, Japan.

A member of the bid monitoring committee of Yamato-city, Kanagawa, Japan, April 2015–present. She lectures to government officials and judges from developing countries at the Training Course on Competition Law and Policy, held by Japan Fair Trade Commission and Japan International Cooperation Agency. She published: Negishi, A., Wakui, M., & Mariyama, N. (eds.) (2022). *Competition law and policy in the Japanese pharmaceutical sector*, Springer.

Ruth TAPLIN is Director of The Centre for Japanese and East Asian Studies, which won Exporter of the Year in Partnership in Trading/Pathfinder for the UK for 2000. She received her doctorate from the London School of Economics and has a GDL in Law. She is the author/editor of 28 books and over 200 articles, wrote freelance for *The Times* newspaper for nine years, and was a consultant to the Federation of Electronics Industry for nine years. For 20 years she has provided translations particularly in Japanese as well as Chinese and Korean for financial and legal documents. Prof. Taplin studied Japanese at Durham University over 25 years ago as part of a special course for future leaders in the Japanese field in the UK. Her recent books published by Routledge include *Intellectual property valuation and innovation: Towards global harmonisation* (2013); *Cyber risk, cyber warfare and IPR theft: Asia, Europe and the*

USA (2021); and *Artificial intelligence, intellectual property, cyber risk and robotics: A new digital age* (2022). She also published *Sustainability: A way forward* (2022), Bloomsbury.

Prof. Taplin is the Founder/Editor of *Interdisciplinary Journal of Economics and Business Law* (www.ijebl.co.uk) now in its fourteenth year. She is owner of the small publishing company CJEAS Ltd. which publishes it.

Kun-lin WU (巫昆霖) is a Part-time Research Fellow, Graduate School of Law, Nagoya University. His fluency in languages includes Taiwanese, Mandarin (native), Japanese (fluent), and English (fluent). His area specialities are Competition Law, Telecommunications Law, and Intellectual Property Law.

Mr. Wu is currently studying for the LLD at Nagoya University, Nagoya, Japan. He received a Bachelor of Laws in the Financial Law program in June 2005, winning the President's Award twice. Wu received his Master of Laws (Economic Law Program) from National Taiwan University (NTU), Taipei, in June 2009. His Master Thesis is entitled, 'From Copyright to Copyleft: An Analysis of Software Licensing Agreements from the Perspective of Interface between Copyright and Competition Law' (in Mandarin).

1 Overview

Ruth Taplin

Introduction

The new digital age technologies have developed rapidly and are presenting challenges to three legal and regulatory areas, which will be interwoven throughout all the chapters and explained in this Overview.

One is competition law whereby the tech giants stifle and crush their competitors to the detriment of other developers of new technology, destroying their Intellectual Property Rights (IPR), chances to develop their own small businesses and customer choice to find an alternative, more effective, cheaper option.

Two, Intellectual Property Rights are infringed through theft of innovations, products by rival companies, nation states, and individual actors. There is overlap here in relation to stealing private data and ideas for anti-competitive purposes in addition to suppressing new inventions of creators on digital platforms, producing junk patents, and using excessive patenting to block competitors.

Three, cyber risk cuts across the other areas in that the more anti-competitive the tech giants are in tandem with IP infringement, the greater is the acceleration of cyber risk.

This book concerns the new central role Competition Law is taking in regulating antitrust and mergers and acquisitions in relation to digital platforms of the tech giants who act as gatekeepers, which is having unforeseen impact on consumer inequality, SME app producers, intellectual property rights, cyber risks, and issues such as AI and data privacy. The essential problem is that Competition Law in all its aspects has not kept pace with the rapid development of digital technology and Artificial Intelligence (AI). It needs to modernise with regulators globally and in unison tackle the growing power and monopolisation of the most dangerous manifestations of digital technology and artificial intelligence, which are embodied in the so-called tech giants such as Google, Amazon, Meta, Microsoft, Apple, and those based in East Asian countries mainly in Japan, China, and South Korea. If not contained and restrained through regulation, the tech giants threaten to become tech monarchies in which wealth and succession becomes inherited with power superseding nation states, straddling the globe interfering in the workings of the nation states, which should be serving the needs of their citizens within a democratic political system. The political systems of tech monarchies are authoritarian

DOI: 10.4324/9781003489542-1

in nature with large swathes of the national population working for them. If we add the nascent, unknown power of AI, especially when controlled by authoritarian political forces, democracy's fragile existence becomes extinguished.

The future problems of reining in tech giants and the subsequent unregulated use of AI are complex and numerous. Tech giants are fully behind 'open access' and 'open source' ways of ultimately benefitting themselves while undermining inventors' and creators' rights to protection of intellectual property rights or nation states' rights to security. Meanwhile they rail against allowing their users to upload their own security applications to protect themselves from installation of malware through tech giants' platforms and pernicious disinformation by state actors. Yet, by allowing users to upload their own security apps, they are challenging tech giants' gatekeeper role to protect users from cyberattack.

A recent example of this conundrum was reflected in recent legislation that was submitted to Congress in the early part of 2022. The two pieces of legislation were the *Open App Markets Act* proposed by Senators Richard Blumenthal (D-Connecticut), Marsha Blackburn (R-Tennessee), and Amy Klobuchar (D-Minnesota). The idea behind it was anti-trust to 'promote competition and reduce gatekeeper power in the app economy, increase choice, improve quality and reduce costs for consumers'.

The second piece of legislation sponsored by Amy Klobuchar of Minnesota and Chuck Grassley (R-Iowa) was the *American Innovation and Choice Online Act.* Such legislation prohibits tech platforms 'favoring their own products or services, disadvantaging rivals, or discriminating among businesses that use their platforms in a manner that would materially harm competition on the platform'. This would allow smartphone users to allow competing app stores onto their mobile phones. Yet, reducing the gatekeeper power of the tech giants and mobile companies through allowing unknown third-party applications to be uploaded by their users can breach user security and even national security.[1]

These two pieces of proposed legislation cannot legally force the tech giants such as Amazon, Google, Apple, or Microsoft to add unscreened applications to their products, but because of the nature of the competition anti-trust element in this legislation, coupled with the tech giants' open access and open-source policies, they would be required to comply while expending great amounts of time, money, and expertise to screen all third-party application uploads. This would need to be done to protect both their own cybersecurity and national security. Additionally, there could be breaches of intellectual property rights as many of the uploaded applications by users could be infringing such rights without understanding they are doing so. Given how Artificial Intelligence and Machine Learning are increasingly being used to facilitate cyberattacks by cybercriminals and state actors, at present and in the future, it can also be used for equal efficiency in predicting and mitigating cyberattacks, adding yet another contradiction.

In 2022, Amazon agreed with European Commission regulators to give merchants operating in the European Union more access to valuable real estate on its website. This ended in part anti-trust investigations by regulators who said the company had used its size and power to stifle competition in the bloc.

Through this settlement, Amazon has avoided a possible multibillion-dollar fine, while giving the European Commission a victory in curtailing the domination of the world's online shopping platform. Additionally, Amazon was also barred from using private non-public information it gathers about independent merchants to inform Amazon's own product choices.

The settlement was an attempt to put more protective measures between Amazon's role as a digital storefront that many businesses, especially small ones, depend on to reach customers, and as a maker of products that often compete with those outside sellers. Such dual roles have created a conflict of interest which allows Amazon to favour its own products and services over smaller competitors who have few other avenues to reach customers online.

Yet, there are possibilities that the new technological breakthroughs such as OpenAI's ChatGPT may open the field for smaller creators and inventors allowing their IP to be protected, such alternatives as search engine Neeva.

'Last year, I was despondent that it was so hard to dislodge the iron grip of Google,' said Sridhar Ramaswamy, who previously oversaw advertising for Google, including Search ads, and now runs Neeva. 'But technological moments like this create an opportunity for more competition.'[2]

For the past 30 years, Netscape's Navigator web browser, Google's search engine, and Apple's iPhone have dominated the technology industry and digital platforms.

Google has itself been for 20 years the premier search engine and gateway to the Internet. It had been complacently dominant until ChatGPT was created through AI technological bot developments, which sounded a red alarm that the new bot could destroy its dominance by replacing traditional search engines.

Google began intensive research that could rival ChatGPT, even though their own researchers assisted with its development, and created LamDA, Language for Dialogue Applications, which was met with great acclaim but Google has been reluctant to make it the main vehicle for Google search because it cannot accommodate digital advertisements which at over 80% comprises, the bulk of Google's revenue stream.

Google is an essential part of this book's enquiry, as in 2024 it has become a test case of how dominant a tech giant can become without regulators trying to challenge its unfair competition practices.

Break Up of Google?

Google has managed to date to resist calls to stop it dominating online search to such an extent that Justice Department officials in the United States the week of the 13 August 2024 found it guilty of violating anti-trust law and asked Federal judges to seek remedies including breaking up Google. The remedies include divesting Google Chrome or the Android smartphone system. Other options include being compelled to share its data with rivals and abandoning deals that make Google the default option on devices such as the iPhone.

Judge Amit P. Mehta is leading the deliberations for the U.S. District Court in the District of Columbia. Judge Mehta, who is overseeing the case, had requested that Google produce a fix for the proposal by 4 September 2024 and a hearing had been set for the 6 September 2024 for the next steps.

Judge Mehta on 5 August 2024 made a landmark ruling that Google had maintained a monopoly over general online search engines and a number of ads that appear in search results. The power of tech giants in the Internet age is being seriously questioned. Other tech giant companies also face antitrust cases including Meta (Facebook and Instagram), Apple, and Amazon, while Google faces another antitrust trial concerning monopolistic practices of ad technology.

The stakes are very high for Google, a US$2 trillion dollar behemoth that generated US$175 billion in revenue from its search engine and other business interests in 2023. Google will appeal any ruling as remedies can have profound effects on the future of the tech giant.

Remedies can have severe effects as shown by a Federal Judge's ruling in 2000 that Microsoft needed to be broken up into separate parts. Upon appeal Microsoft was never split but other aspects of the remedies meant that Microsoft's dominance ended, opening the doors to new market entries such as Google.

Of available remedies, Judge Mehta could demand that Google divest Chrome, its web browser, or Android, its software for smartphones, as both of these products use Google as the automatic search engine, which supports the company's dominance. Another tool it could be requested to divest is one that runs text ads in search.[3]

In September 2024 the Google monopolistic Ad Technology trial, which took place in the U.S. District Court for the Eastern District of Virginia, lasted about four weeks, then Judge Leonie Brinkema can take several months to make a decision. The stakes are high: The U.S. government has asked for a breakup of the company, requiring Google to sell off some assets.

Several major themes emerged during the trial. The government alleges that Google has illegally built and maintained its monopoly and explains how those practices have harmed website operators, advertisers, and ultimately consumers. The Justice Department's main arguments are the following:

Google built a monopoly in ad tech software. The Justice Department and a group of states accused the tech company of abusing control of its ad technology and violating antitrust law, partly through its 2008 acquisition of the advertising software company DoubleClick. Since this purchase, Google has pushed up ad prices and also harmed publishers by taking a big cut of each sale.

The acquisition of DoubleClick 'set the competitive conditions for all the anticompetitive conduct that followed', according to Julia Tarver Wood, the government's lead courtroom lawyer. The government has stated that Google controls 87 per cent of the market for a crucial technology that publishers use to sell ads.

The DoubleClick acquisition gave Google a competitive edge in its ad tech operation. The first is a system that people who run websites use to offer ad space, like the rectangle at the top of the homepage on a news site. The second is a so-called exchange – software that conducts real-time auctions between publishers and advertisers to sell ads as users load a web page. Google also monopolises some technology that allows advertisers to buy ad space on different websites.

In real terms this means that Google can be involved in every stage of a deal to sell ad space online. The Justice Department pointed to an email from a former Google employee that compared that arrangement to allowing a bank to own the New York Stock Exchange.

Google's ad tech business generated US$31 billion in revenue last year, which amounted to roughly a tenth of the company's total revenues.

Google also rigged the rules of the auctions to benefit itself, according to the government. That included, at various times, self-preferencing itself when publishers compared bids from ad space from different auction systems.

Google harmed publishers, advertisers and consumers by charging a 20 per cent fee to publishers who run ad auctions using its system, known as an ad exchange which the government said had been possible only because of Google's dominance.

To accommodate that fee, advertisers paid more than they would have otherwise in a free market, and publishers made less, with Google skimming the high fee off the top of each transaction. The government says that means the public has ultimately suffered, as the websites where they get news and information have been bled dry of revenue and higher ad prices made products cost more.

'It is likely that consumers were harmed', Dr Rosa M. Abrantes-Metz, an expert witness for the government, said during the testimony. Monopoly harms consumers because the merchant fees are ultimately passed along through higher prices across myriad purchases, Attorney General Merrick Garland argued.[4]

Meanwhile in the United Kingdom, the Competition and Markets Authority (CMA) has decided that Google is using anti-competitive practices to dominate advertising technology which most likely could be harming thousands of UK publishers and advertisers.[5]

On Monday, 7 October 2024, Judge James Donato of the U.S. District Court for the Northern District of California ordered Google to initiate a series of changes to address its anticompetitive conduct. For three years starting 1st November, Google must allow developers to bring their own app stores to the Android mobile operating system. It must also allow app makers to charge users with their own billing systems, outside the Android ecosystem.

Google will be entitled to charge developers 'a reasonable fee for these services', but the charges must be based on Google's actual costs with transparency.

In his ruling, Judge Donato wrote, 'Google's modus operandi in this case has been to deluge the court in an ocean of comments, many of which were cursory and undeveloped.'

Epic, the maker of the popular video game Fortnite, savoured this victory, as it has waged legal battles against Google and Apple since 2020 in an attempt to weaken their power over the app economy. Epic had petitioned the court to open Google's Android system so it could offer its own app store while avoiding the company's rules and fees. Judge Donato's ruling fulfilled most of those requests, but will still force Epic and other developers to pay Google for Android's security and content moderation services.[6]

Maintaining Google's Gatekeeping Role in Relation to Security

Why did Judge Donato continue to require Epic and other developers to continue to pay fees to Google for Androids security and content moderation services?

In our estimation, it was to secure the positive and expansive ability to block potential cyberattacks and massive attempts at disinformation that only Google would be able to do because of its size and sophistication, much like Microsoft and Apple, which can block harmful cyberattacks in all its forms through its gatekeeping roles.

However, this has not stopped Google from trying to dominate the current AI smartphone market. This move into consumer hardware by merging their teams that work with Android and the team developing Pixel phones, such as Pixel 9 and Pixel 9 Pro XL, were available for pre-order on the 22 August and 4 September 2024 before Apple's AI featured smartphones.[7]

European Union: The Most Active Regulator

The European Union has been emerging in recent years as one of the most aggressive regulators to rein in tech giants globally. In December 2022, Amazon agreed after an investigation of its antitrust practices to allow access to its digital storefront platform, which smaller merchants rely on to sell their products. The dual roles as mentioned above created a conflict of interest that allowed Amazon to favour its own products on digital platforms over smaller rivals that depend on sales from the very same digital platforms. Amazon was also at this time barred from gathering non-public information about merchants who use their digital platforms to inform their own product choices. Amazon also agreed to let outside sellers to partake in its Prime programme, even if they do not use Amazon's logistics business.

The e-commerce tech giant agreed to these changes to avoid US$billions in fines and further investigations/lawsuits by the European Commission under Margrethe Vestager, the European Commissioner's Executive Vice-President, who was in charge of digital policy and antitrust to allow enforcement. Vestager viewed the settlements as a win-win situation for smaller retailers and consumers.

Amazon announced that it was pleased with most of the agreement and that its online digital platforms can continue to accommodate the 225,000 small and medium sized businesses selling through their online stores.

In 2022 European antitrust regulators brought charges against Meta for anticompetitive practices concerning its marketplace position for selling goods and threatened to fine it billions. At the same time the regulators were beginning to investigate Apple and Google for similar anticompetitive practices.

Big Tech companies began in 2022 to comply with European antitrust laws that would take effect in 2024 and follow rules that negate anticompetitive business practices including unacceptable user generated content on social media.[8]

Antitrust Outcomes for 2024

The outcomes and remedies that have been meted out to Google in 2024 for its unfair competition practices in relation to the attempts to dominate and exclude or give unfair access to digital platforms have been described earlier in this chapter.

The case of Apple were still ongoing in 2024 and concern some very serious breaches of antitrust law rules. European Union regulators have claimed that Apple has breached new digital competition laws by instituting rules in its App Store marketplace which prevents other app makers from directing users to less expensive options elsewhere.

A preliminary investigation was carried out by the European Commission that found Apple in breach of the Digital Markets Act (DMA) through suppressing competition. The DMA came into effect in March 2024, as an attempt to prevent tech companies from dominating digital markets. This is the first time that EU regulators have used the new rules to deal with a tech giant. The new laws stipulate that app developers cannot be blocked from informing users about less expensive options and promotions offered outside an app store, as Apple rules have prevented this.

Per the DMA, if Apple is found guilty of breaching these rules, it could face a fine up to 10 per cent of its global annual revenue of US$383.3 billion and if the offence is repeated, 20 per cent. Apple has made changes to its EU app store, allowing apps to be downloaded from other websites and third-party app stores onto its devices. Margrethe Vestager hailed the European Commission's new rules as yet another step ensuring that Apple and other tech giants will comply with the demand that outside app developers are allowed to communicate freely with their own users. The European Commission in addition opened a new investigation into the fees that they charge app developers, which includes a core technology fee of $0.50 per download if their app is used by more than a million people. The regulator also questioned the fees Apple charges for the developers' initial acquisition of new customers.

Apple will be able to respond to the regulators findings, which will be assessed before the European Commission makes a final decision on the case by March 2025.[9]

Europe's determination to show Big Tech companies that they cannot escape paying for breaches of unfair competition in their gatekeeping role is backed up by large fines. In March 2024, Apple was fined by the European Commission £1.54 billion for stifling competition in music streaming, in this case Spotify. This was a marked change to Apple's anticompetitive practice of not allowing Spotify to advertise in-app promotion or discounts. It has been an ongoing contention between the two fiercely competitive music streaming rivals. Daniel Ek, the Swedish founder of Spotify, argued that Apple has been obliterating competition by including a 30 per cent fee on in-app sales for companies on the store. Ek said, 'They won't charge 30 per cent (the App Store fee) to their own music service, so they should allow us not to pay 30 per cent so we can compete on a level playing field'.[10]

The power of the DMA was certainly proved in the Apple/Spotify case. It is well known that Margrethe Vestager is the determined instigator of EU rules that challenge the tech giant's dominance and was the US tech nemesis. Vestager ended her term in 2024, with Teresa Ribera Rodriguez, the Spanish official, decided as her successor. Whether Ribera will exhibit the same drive and determination is unknown, but the modernisation of Competition Law emanating from the European Commission will most likely not lose its momentum under the DMA.[11]

The UK; Competition as the Key Driver of Innovation

The UK Competition Markets Authority (CMA), under the direction of Chief Executive Sarah Cardell, rather than setting a tone of determination like Margarethe Vestager is exhibiting caution and risk aversion that is viewed by some as stifling innovation and competition in UK markets. The case of Vodaphone in June 2024 when Chief Executive Margherita Dalle Valle put forward her plan for an £18 billion merger with the UK's Three, the CMA decided to investigate, dragging out the possible deal.

In April 2024, the CMA's decision to block Microsoft's US$69 billion takeover of Activision Blizzard, the maker of *Call of Duty,* was questioned as a move that could harm the British economy. Additionally, the European Commission the following month granted permission for this deal to take place, which made the EU look open for business while the UK appeared closed. This decision was in contradistinction to other CMA decisions. In the case of Meta in 2023, the CMA ordered Meta to sell Giphy, an animation business that resulted in the tech giant expected to pay US$400 million for the company, divest it for a mere US$53 million, while in 2024, the regulator supported Amazon's US$17 billion purchase of robotic vacuum cleaner company iRobot. The CMA decision in this case was viewed as less controversial because iRobot had a low market share.

The regulator gave the impression in a number of other acquisitions that it was a hindrance to economic growth. Amazon took a 16 per cent stake in Deliveroo for US$575 million. Clearance by the CMA took over a year which meant William Shu, the founder of Deliveroo, had to fire 30 per cent of his team and almost ran out of cash.

The Regulatory Reform Group, Westminster body has been calling for a joint committee that consists of both peers and MPs to look at regulators to ensure they have a responsibility to economic growth. Sarah Cardell has insisted the CMA is dedicated to both innovation and growth, while being seen in action to dispute the idea that enforcing open and fair competition is a driver of innovation and growth.[12]

Where Competition Law and Intellectual Property Intersect

Lina Khan, the past Chair of the US Federal Trade Commission (USFTC), began her career by challenging and carrying out investigations concerning the practice of junk patents in the pharmaceutical industries in the US. Big Pharma, as a similar but different pharmaceutical version of tech giants, have been engaged in excessive patenting to block competitors from creating generic products and being listed in the *Approved Drug Products with Therapeutic Equivalence*, or Orange Book.

This meant for example, that Teva Pharmaceuticals and nine other companies made small tweaks to their patented medical devices such as inhalers used by those with asthma to prolong their patents and stifle competition from generic pharmaceutical companies. Teva charged hundreds of dollars for their inhalers in the US, but sell them at a fraction of the cost, such as US$35, overseas. A number of Senators and Representatives of Congress such as Senator Elizabeth Warren were less than pleased that Teva was using patent law to support themselves in artificially raising prices on lifesaving medication in the US under the auspices of Federally funded programmes such as Medicare for the elderly and those in poverty.[13] The Teva example is alluded to in Addendum Chapter 6 of this book in relation to the European Commission and excessive patenting and anticompetitive practices.

The Orange Book puts generic companies on notice of certain types of patents that a brand company claims covers its product. Patents listed in the Orange Book must claim the reference listed drug or a method of using it. By listing patents, brand drug manufacturers may benefit from a 30-month stay of Federal Drug Administration (FDA) approval of generic drug applications, regardless of whether a court ultimately finds the patent at issue, is valid, or infringed by the competing product. Orange Book listing abuse is strictly a harmful practice of pharmaceutical regulation rather than the patent system as a whole.

Big Pharma is akin to Big Tech, but Pharma is slightly different in that it uses the Orange Book and other means to exclude generic pharmaceutical competition in a manner that harms consumers, SME companies, and alternative creative inventors who wish to patent their invention. The US Federal Trade Commission (FTC) attempts to scrutinise carefully those Pharma companies listed on the Orange Book for anticompetitive practices.[14]

The Modernisation of Competition Law

In the case of Google, it is attempting to take part in the modernisation of Competition Law by advancing new ways to work in tandem with the local community rather than competing against it. Tech giants such as Google have been through unfair competition, destroying local news that used to flourish before Big Tech took through open access all news stories and local advertising revenue. Now, in a new scheme in California with Governor Newsom's consent, they have agreed to fund local newsrooms, which have been closing, with a US$250 million boost which means more local journalists could be hired while working with A New Transformation Fund administered by the Graduate School of Journalism at the University of California, Berkeley. The aim is to promote local journalism with 12 per cent of funding reserved for them and underrepresented groups. Funding for the first five years will come with an initial US$30 million and US$10 million per annum after that. Google will contribute US$15 million with remaining payments per annum of roughly US$10 million. This proposal has been welcomed but also criticised for doing too little with inadequate resources.

President pro tempore of the State Senate, Michael McQuire, summarised these concerns: 'We have concerns that this proposal lacks sufficient funding for newspapers and local media, and doesn't fully address the inequities facing the industry', said Senator McGuire, a Democrat. He added that 'the Senate was pursuing a global solution that would hold all of these companies accountable'.[15]

Do Rigorous Antitrust Laws Work?

In Japan, the Act on Improvement of Transparency and Fairness in Trading on Specified Digital Platforms (Transparency and Fairness Act) (Act no. 38, 03.06.2020) was instituted on 1 February 2021, which is designed to ensure transparency to achieve fairness with respect to digital platform operators and to ensure fair and free competition in digital markets. The Act designates digital platform businesses whose transparency and fairness in trading should be improved as 'specified digital platform providers', thereby, such specified providers, whether they are domestic or overseas businesses, are to be subject to certain rules. The Act requires specified digital platform providers to disclose their information, e.g., terms and conditions of trading and give prior notice of any change thereof to the platform users. Yet, this Act also falls short of a comprehensive antitrust law as do subsequent antitrust laws as argued in Chapter 3 of this book.

Antitrust cases in relation to attempts to dominate use of digital platforms in regards to access by creators, choice for consumers, intellectual property infringement, and increased risk of cyberattack have increased substantially since we began this book project. There are old cases still waiting to be decided and new ones that attempt to modernise the regulation of competition laws in Japan, South Korea, the UK, EU, and the USA. Some are interrelated internationally and others are standalone national cases.

What is new is that South Korea in mid-February 2024 unleashed through the Korean Federal Trade Commission (KFTC) with the backing of President Yoon Suk Yeol, the toughest competition laws outside Europe to protect its online platforms from tech giants' dominance of both international and domestic (chaebol-linked) Internet conglomerates. What the KFTC did not expect was the tremendous backlash by lobbyists and consumers.

The second noteworthy trend is that despite a basically healthy economy, Japan has entered into recession and slipped into fourth place behind Germany in terms of the size of its economy. One of the main reasons for this is a substantial drop in consumer spending. When Japanese consumers rein in spending, they signify what the problem is such as with many failed consumption taxes that were levied by the Japanese government. In this case today, it appears that the drop in consumer spending can be linked to ineffective and outdated competition laws.

Competition Law is currently seen as a vehicle for reducing consumer inequality and poverty, a role not previously contemplated. The EU/UK is leading such legislation with Japan not far behind and the US making important regulatory contributions. Very little is known and has been written about this topic in the English language in relation to Japan, China, and South Korea. This edited volume would therefore, make a unique contribution to the current literature. The most burning issue that this book will confront and analyse is that Competition

Law in its present form is unable to deal with the new advances in digital technology that have made private sector tech giants not subject to national jurisdictions as they straddle the world, leaving national regulators ill-equipped to curtail their unfair competitive excesses. Therefore, the gatekeeping role of digital platforms has broken through the boundaries of national regulation and pushed its ability to break antitrust law with impunity pursuing unfair practice to its own advantage.

How the tech giants use their digital platforms to their own unfair advantage vis-à-vis the regulators, nation states, consumers, and SME companies is analysed in the following chapters. How regulators, nation states, consumers, and companies deal with the need to expand Competition Laws to include the new threats to unfair practices are assessed in particular in Japan, China, UK, EU, and USA. Each of these regions of the world has unique contributions and challenges in modernising their Competition Laws to deal with such unprecedented dominance of digital platforms by the tech giants. Japan, is especially, caught in the middle of these challenges. In relation to the other geopolitical regions while in Europe, Brexit has caused the UK to find solutions independent of the EU. However, as noted above, how severe must national regulators legislate new antitrust laws to make them effective? Is it large fines or exclusion from markets themselves that will cause tech giants to change their anticompetitive practices?

The other crucial issue is how can tech giants be effectively persuaded to open their digital platforms for fair use that benefits consumers, SMEs, and creators while allowing tech giants to maintain their important role as keepers of digital security that protects all users from cyberattacks and content misinformation. This essential aim to tackle this issue which poses a conundrum is yet to be solved fully and will be addressed in this book from various perspectives in each chapter.

Ongoing, Partially Resolved and Resolved Cases to Date

Antitrust cases in relation to attempts to dominate use of digital platforms in regards to access by creators, choice for consumers, intellectual property infringement, and increased risk of cyberattack have increased substantially since we began this book project. There are old cases still waiting to be decided and new ones that attempt to modernise the regulation of competition laws in Japan, China, South Korea, the UK, EU, and the USA. Some are inter-related internationally and others are standalone national cases. Some examples are the following.

The United States has some of the largest and potentially effective cases that will curtail the worst excesses of tech giants in using their digital platform dominance for unfair competition. The Federal Government as of October 2024 has five active cases against four tech giants – Google, Amazon, Apple, and Meta – which are slowly moving forward according to the strength of objections by the behemoths who are finding it difficult to win the monopolisation cases. The latest updates have been made throughout this chapter and in subsequent chapters of this book. Briefly, some of the cases that show the extent of severity and range of issues are the following.

In October 2023, the USFTC sued Amazon for illegal practices which allege that Amazon abuses its market dominance to lock its third-party retailers into its selling platform to use services such as its ads which stops rivals in such a way that it raises prices and reduces consumer choice. It has been seen as a landmark case, which a former US regulator stated was the most important case in its 109-year history. This case and related ones are ongoing and require following through the course of the book.

From October 2023, *United States* v *Google LLC* has been the biggest market dominance case since Microsoft in the 1990s, as Google is the automatically installed default search engine.

In February 2024, Indonesian President Joko Widodo signed a regulation requiring tech giant digital platforms to pay media outlets that provide them with content, which aims to level the playing field between the media industry and Big Tech companies.

In December 2023, the *New York Times* initiated a lawsuit against Open AI (ChatGPT) and Microsoft, its backer, concerning copyright for AI and content creators.

This case and others represent just some of the issues being dealt with in this book.

Overview of All Chapters

The other chapters in this book, which address the modernisation of Competition Law with current regulations that are reining in the increased powers of the tech giants to dominate the digital platforms, cover different aspects with an emphasis on Japan, Britain, Europe, and the United States, which are homes to the most powerful tech giants. A chapter on China is also included to provide a contrast of what constitutes competition law regulation for tech giants in a non-democratic, authoritarian political system.

In Chapter 2, co-editor Kazuhiko Fuchikawa argues that the utilisation of AI and algorithms by digital platformers should not be condemned in and of itself, as it holds the potential to achieve efficiency by offering new products and services. However, competition law's evaluation of new exclusionary practices that cannot be fully regulated under existing competition laws has become a significant issue.

For instance, by understanding consumer preferences based on collected big data and utilising AI and algorithms, personalised pricing conditions can be set, creating new demand. However, this also carries the possibility of surplus transfer from consumers with a higher willingness to pay to consumers with a lower willingness to pay. It can also potentially impact the distribution of surplus between consumers and manufacturers. In this way, personalised pricing refers to the practice of businesses setting different prices for each consumer or consumer group (for the same product or service) based on their characteristics and behaviours, ensuring that the prices correspond to their respective estimated willingness to pay.

In addition, digital platformers may play a dual role by participating in competition themselves, allowing monopolistic digital platformers to potentially abuse their dominant position in the digital platform market they operate, enabling them to compete on more favourable terms than their competitors. In this manner, the self-preferencing practice refers to the exertion of market dominance by monopolistic entities as leverage in a specific market, causing anti-competitive effects in closely related markets that are difficult to regulate effectively within the conventional framework of competition law.

Therefore, this chapter examines competition law's evaluation of AI and algorithm configuration and modification by digital platformers from a comparative legal perspective, considering the regulations of competition law in Japan, the US, and Europe in order to explore appropriate means of regulation. The impact of AI algorithms is not limited to economic activities. The emergence of Generative AI has influenced freedom of expression and creative activities, significantly affecting journalists and freelancers.

In Chapter 3, Kentaro Hirayama assesses fair competition and appropriate data use in the digital platform business in Japan, which is the second most populous country in the G7 after the United States and which has experienced a unique development of digital platform businesses since the dawn of the Internet era. However, in recent years, globally fast-growing Big Tech companies such as GAFA (Google, Amazon, Facebook, and Apple) have begun to gain dominant positions in certain service sectors in Japan. Through the collection of various data such as personal information and the application of advanced algorithms to such big data, these US and Japanese platform business operators have intensified competition in Japan. In addition, business collaborations between Japanese and US companies, such as Yahoo Japan's adoption of Google's search engine for its search service, are also increasing. These circumstances have made the issues that need to be examined in order to ensure fair competition – a goal of competition law policy – increasingly complex.

In this chapter, the author, who has experience as a lawyer and an examiner at Japan's competition authority, analyses notable cases in Japan's platform business from a practical perspective. These cases are (i) the business cooperation between Yahoo Japan and Google, (ii) the merger between Yahoo Japan and LINE Corporation – a dominant company in the messenger service sector, (iii) a lawsuit by a restaurant against a restaurant rating company for exploitative practices, and (iv) the formal investigation against Airbnb Japan by the Japan's competition authority.

In addition, this chapter will also present the Japanese government's monitoring scheme for the actions of Big Tech companies such as GAFA and Yahoo Japan (where the author is a monitoring board member) and cases where corrective guidance has been provided under this scheme. Through these discussions, this chapter aims to propose a set of principles for fair competition and appropriate data use in the platform business sector that could be adopted globally.

In Chapter 4, Shuya Hayashi and Kun-lin Wu concentrate on cloud computing which lays a competition foundation for all digital services because it provides companies with access to infrastructure, platform, and software 'as a service'. Given the low running costs and flexibility, individuals and companies tend to choose third-party cloud service providers (CSPs) instead of deploying their own on-premise private cloud. CSPs thus play a crucial role in the digital sector, and how they affect competition therein should be analysed not only in terms of relevant markets (e.g., infrastructure as a service (IaaS), platform as a service (PaaS), and software as a service (SaaS)), but also from the perspective of a digital ecosystem. Particularly, the high switching costs (data transfer costs, if technically possible) may lead to vendor lock-in, which limits competition. In view of this situation, the Digital Markets Act (DMA) includes cloud computing in its definition of core platform services (Art. 2(2), Point (g)). Numerous competition and regulatory authorities have been actively conducting market studies in the cloud service sector to identify potential competition issues. For instance, the Japan Fair Trade Commission (JFTC) conducted a survey in 2022 regarding trade practices in the cloud service sector to identify a) the trade practices involving dominant digital platform providers and b) the state of competition in the cloud service sector. Another recent example is British telecom regulator OFCOM's (Office of Communications) interim report, *Cloud Services Market Study*, which was published in April 2023. This chapter thus seeks to review these legislations and market studies and to provide recommendations with a view to promoting competition in the digital sector. Intellectual Property Rights and any cyber risk implications are included.

In Chapter 5, Xiaofei Lu looks at Competition Law and the tech giants in China. China's fast-growing digital economy coincides with the expansion of tech giants like Alibaba and Tencent. Despite their significant influence, concerns over competition law have grown. This chapter investigates the relationship between competition law and large tech companies in China.

Initially, China's competition law is examined, especially antitrust law, assessing its history, current status, and trends, considering social, cultural, economic, and industrial policies. Next, the governance structures and decision-making processes of China's major tech companies are explored, identifying their operational realities and competitive challenges. Specific cases are analysed, such as Alibaba's anti-trust violations, to understand China's competition law's real objectives, effectiveness, and impact on tech company growth. Appropriate laws and regulations are proposed from an international perspective to maintain fair competition without hampering tech companies' development, discussing how such companies should respond to these laws and regulations including intellectual property rights and any issues of cyber risk.

In Chapter 6, the Addendum, Naoko Mariyama, elaborates on competition law and intellectual property rights infringement by Big Pharma and Big Tech in relation to excessive patenting. This is relevant for the future as Big Tech is entering the healthcare sector and Big Pharma must have modern antitrust laws to deal with the encroachment of Big Tech and the exploitation of excessive patenting.

Big Tech giants wield considerable power, and their actions may potentially violate competition laws by excluding competitors as described in previous chapters in relation to unfair practices on digital platforms. However, it is important to note that the mere exclusion of competitors does not always constitute a violation of competition law, as competition inherently involves eliminating rivals. Nevertheless, if a dominant company were to acquire numerous patents for a single product with the intention of preventing new entrants, could this conduct infringe upon competition law? Big Pharma has its own massive companies that operate in a different marketplace with its own rules, but this is changing and the link between intellectual property practices and unfair competition are akin to such practices found on digital platforms.

Research has revealed that excessive patenting is endemic to the pharmaceutical industry. Indeed, technology giants have already invaded the healthcare sector, with excessive patenting, becoming a powerful vehicle to exclude competition in a harmful way as outlined in this chapter.

In Chapter 7, the Conclusion, Ruth Taplin analyses the future of Competition Law in the regions assessed in relation to modernising to address new challenges brought about by the expansion of digital technology and the anti-competitive nature of tech giants' gatekeeper role on their digital platforms. The success of new regulations in the regions will be addressed, in addition to the complexities of conceiving regulation that maintains a fair and balanced marketplace that allows tech giants to act as important gatekeepers, which maintains security practices that do not facilitate cyberattack and content misinformation while opening their digital platforms to other App providers in safety and invention.

Notes

1 Ruth Taplin, *Artificial Intelligence Intellectual Property, Cyber Risk and Robotics; A New Digital Age,* 'Conclusion', (Abingdon; Routledge, 2023).
2 Nico Grant, Cade Metz, 'A New Chat Bot Is a "Code Red" for Google's Search Business', *New York Times*, 12 December 2022.
3 David McCabe and Nico Grant, 'Google Debuts A.I.-Powered Phones in Latest Attempt to Best the iPhone', *New York Times,* 13 August 2024.
4 David McCabe, 'What the U.S. Has Argued in the Google Ad Tech Antitrust Trial', *New York Times*, 20 September 2024.
5 Chris Vallance, 'Google Abusing Ad Tech Dominance, UK Competition Watchdog Finds', BBC Online, 6 September 2024.
6 Nico Grant, 'Google Must Open Android to Other App Stores and Billing Options, Judge Rules', *New York Times*, 7 October 2024.
7 Nico Grant, 'Google Debuts A.I.-Powered Phones in Latest Attempt to Best the iPhone', *New York Times*, 13 August 2024.
8 Adam Sartariano, 'Amazon and E.U. Reach Deal to End Antitrust Investigation', *New York Times*, 20 December 2022.
9 Emma Taggart, 'Apple Broke EU Competition Rules', *The Times,* 25 June 2024.
10 Katie Prescott, 'Spotify Victory over Apple in App Store Fight', *The Times,* 25 January 2024.
11 Katie Prescott, 'Big Tech Be Warned, Europe Means Business with Tough New Stance', *The Times*, 6 March 2024.
12 Alex Ralph and Katie Prescott, 'Competition Regulator Is Taking Fire from All Sides', *The Times*, 19 June 2023.
13 Dan Diamond, 'FTC Opens Investigation into Teva, Escalating Patent Fight with Pharma Industry', *The Washington Post*, 1 July 2024.
14 https://www.ftc.gov/system/files/ftc_gov/pdf/p239900orangebookpolicystatement092023.pdf
15 Karen Eise and Shawn Hubler, 'Google Joins $250 Million Deal to Support Newsrooms in California', *The New York Times,* 21 August 2024.

2 Regulating Non-Price Exclusionary Conducts and Preferential Treatments in the Digital Economy

Kazuhiko Fuchikawa

In the digital economy, once a monopolistic market situation is established, there is a risk that market self-correcting mechanisms may not function properly, and barriers to entry could be formed.[1] In addition, interaction can occur between several complementary markets and sectors. Such interaction refers to an 'ecosystem,' analogous to the ecology of the natural world. Ecosystems refer to the interactions of communities of firms, upstream components and downstream complements, and the interactions between platforms and complementary products or services that make platforms valuable as a hub in a multi-sided market.[2]

The ecosystem in the digital economy, while providing convenience to users, raises concerns that users may become locked into the ecosystem due to increasing dependency on services within the ecosystem, allowing ecosystem operators to maintain a monopolistic position.[3] Ecosystems can be categorised into two types: (1) those in which multiple independent businesses form a consortium, and (2) in which multiple products or services provided by a single business entity are aggregated.[4]

These products and services may be substitutable (e.g. Messenger and WhatsApp by Facebook (Meta)) or complementary (e.g. Apple devices and iOS). In some cases, it may also be difficult to separate products or services.[5]

Digital platform operators often engage in businesses that are complementary to each other. The digital platform businesses of Big Tech companies mutually interact, forming an ecosystem that may lead to a monopolistic market.[6] In the digital ecosystems where complementary businesses interact with each other and form multiple layers, while the SSNIP (small but significant and non-transitory increase in price) test was adequate in the past, it is now insufficient for evaluating competitive harm, such as foreclosure and exclusionary conduct, in today's multi-layered ecosystem.[7]

A certain consensus has been fostered across legal jurisdictions (EU, East Asia, USA) with respect to the regulation of collusion under competition laws. In contrast, the approach for the new type of exclusionary conduct such as self-preferencing, personalised pricing[8], and ranking manipulation[9] varies across different jurisdictions. As for the regulation of unilateral conduct, there is a growing concern over whether the new type of exclusionary conduct constitutes exclusionary or exploitative behaviour and should be deemed illegal under competition law. The regulation

DOI: 10.4324/9781003489542-2

of these practices, especially self-preferencing, is currently regulated separately in each country's legal jurisdiction with different protocols. While some competition authorities actively regulate self-preferencing, others do not.

Self-preferencing refers to the practice of giving preferential treatment to one's own products or services over those of a third party.[10] In self-preferential treatment, the platform operator plays a 'dual role', acting not only as an intermediary but also as a seller.[11] Self-preferencing can be broadly categorised into three types: (i) manipulation of search engine results, (ii) manipulation of ranking on the platforms, and (iii) use of transaction data from third-party sellers.[12] However, it appears that all three categories are not necessarily mutually exclusive or fully comprehensive. Self-preferencing is considered in some cases to resemble practices such as tying, refusal to deal, and exclusive dealing.[13] By engaging in self-preferencing in the ecosystem, a company may improve the perceived quality of its own products or services and gain a better reputation.[14] On the other hand, self-preferencing may exclude competitors or deter new entrants.

Self-preferencing is regulated mainly in legal jurisdictions with laws involving the abuse of a dominant position. For instance, the Google Shopping case[15] and the Amazon Buy Box case[16] in the EU can be cited as precedent setting examples of self-preferencing.[17] However, in jurisdictions that emphasise freedom of choice for all businesses including large corporations to choose their trading partners, there is not necessarily an obligation to help competitors.[18]

In the USA, there is concern that labelling practices as 'self-preferencing' could obscure the competitive analysis. Therefore, the US has taken the position that the regulation of 'self-preferencing'-like conduct should focus only on exclusionary conduct by firms with market power.[19] Therefore, the US continues to regulate conduct that may constitute self-preferencing only after market power and anticompetitive effects are established.

Even in the US, where there is a more cautious approach to regulating self-preferencing, it is acknowledged that competition law will apply when self-preferencing leads to exclusionary conduct. This raises the question; when self-preferencing results in exclusionary conduct, will there be any difference from the existing theory of harm under competition law across different jurisdictions? If so, what are the differences?

This chapter examines the practice of platform operators who give preferential treatment to their own products or services over those of a third party and analyses whether these practices extend the scope of exclusionary conduct as a result of self-preferencing.

There is a need to expand the scope of exclusionary conduct that is deemed illegal in cases involving self-preferencing in platform markets within ecosystems. However, the question arises: What should be the legal limit?

The purpose of this chapter is to clarify the scope of self-preferencing through comparative studies and to identify the challenges in regulating the practice of preferencing one's own products or services in the ecosystem.[20] To achieve this, the chapter examines a series of Google cases, including the Google Android case and Google Ad case, which have raised common competition law issues in the US, the

EU, and Japan through preferential treatment. This chapter then examines the relationship between exclusionary conduct and self-preferencing, as well as the possibility of expanding the scope of exclusionary conduct due to preferential treatment.

Regulation of Non-Price Exclusionary Conduct

Self-preferencing is regulated through ex-ante regulation such as the EU's Digital Market Act[21] and the Japanese Act on Promotion of Competition for Specified Smartphone Software.[22] Given the dominant position of certain Big Tech companies, it is reasonable to apply ex-ante regulations to self-preferencing. In contrast, under competition law, which functions as an ex-post regulation, self-preferencing is typically examined through established exclusionary conduct such as tying, refusal to deal, or exclusive dealing, or it may be considered a new form of exclusionary conduct.

This section will first analyse the Google Shopping case, a leading precedent on self-preferencing, to clarify its meaning. Second, it will address non-price preferential treatment, focusing on tying and exclusive dealing.

The Google Shopping case stands as the leading precedent for addressing self-preferencing in the digital sector, which involves non-price preferential treatment under traditional competition law frameworks.

In *Google Shopping,*[23] the Commission determined that Google abused its dominant position in the general search market and specific product search maker. Google provided preferential treatment to its own comparison shopping sites by positioning them prominently. In contrast, competing comparison shopping sites were relegated to less visible positions. These competing sites were displayed in blue text, and Google's algorithms lowered their ranking. As a result, the Commission imposed a fine of more than €2.4 billion on Google. It also found that traffic from 'general search' result accounts for the majority of traffic to competing comparison shopping sites, and these sites could not be replaced by other available comparison shopping sites at that time.[24] Google's conduct led to cessation of services provided by these comparison shopping sites.

Google appealed to the General Court. In 2021, the GC dismissed most of Google's claim but upheld the Commission's decision. However, the GC found that the Commission did not adequately establish abuse in the market for online general services.[25] The GC held that leveraging by a dominant undertaking itself does not infringe Article 102 of the Treaty on the Functioning of the European Union (TFEU). However, certain types of leveraging, such as bundling and the refusal to supply interoperability information, as seen in *Microsoft*, may infringe the TFEU. Moreover, regarding the scope of the special responsibility of dominant undertakings, it must be considered in light of the specific circumstances of each case which one show that competition has been weakened.[26] The GC also noted that Google's general search results page possesses characteristics similar to those of an essential facility.[27]

Google appealed to the European Court of Justice (ECJ),[28] seeking to annul both the General Court's judgement and the Commission's decision. The ECJ emphasised that the purpose of the provision is to prevent competition from being restricted to the detriment of individual undertakings and consumers, by sanctioning the conduct of the undertakings with dominant position that hinders competition on the merits.[29] The ECJ pointed out that Article 102 TFEU does not sanction the existence per se of dominant position, but only abusive exploitation of the dominant position.[30]

The ECJ highlighted two circumstances. First Google favours its own services by positioning and displaying them more prominently on its general results pages than those of results from competing comparison shopping services, which deviates competition on the merits. Second, Google simultaneously demotes results of competing comparison shopping services by an adjustment algorithm. These circumstances enabled Google's practices to be placed in the context of the two relevant markets and the functioning of competition on those markets, and were thus capable of demonstrating potential exclusionary effects on the downstream market. The ECJ concluded that Google's conduct is discriminative and deviates competition on the merits with specific situations.[31]

Google Shopping and Self-Preferencing

The ECJ clarified the scope of Article 102 TFEU; it is not limited to abusive practices relating to indispensable goods and service; and that the principles established in *Bronner* (C-7/97, EU:C:1998:568) do not apply to all exclusionary practices.[32] The ECJ suggested that Google's practice constitutes an independent form of leveraging abuse.[33]

The ECJ emphasised that it is necessary to demonstrate, using methods other than those of competition on the merits, that such conduct has the actual or potential effect of restricting competition by excluding equally efficient competing undertakings from the relevant market(s) or by hindering their growth of those markets.[34]

The ECJ did not explicitly refer to 'self-preferencing'. It cannot be definitively stated that 'self-preferencing' constitutes an independent form of abusive practice. Instead, the ECJ characterised Google's conduct as 'leveraging abuse', although Attorney General Juliane Kokott explicitly mentioned 'self-preferencing'.

Regarding self-preferencing, there are both pros and cons to regulating it, even within the EU.[35] As such, self-preferencing is not inherently illegal by object; rather, an effects-based approach is taken. Ultimately, it can be said that self-preferencing is regulated as a new form of exclusionary practice when the dominant digital platform undertakings favour their own products or services by positioning or displaying them more prominently while demoting those of competitors in the downstream market, leading to, at the very least, a potential exclusionary effect, as a foreclosure.[36]

Tying

As mentioned earlier, abusive practices including self-preferencing are not confined to refusal to access, therefore 'indispensability' is not a decisive factor for self-preferencing. Self-preferencing is sometimes said to be akin to tying and refusal to deal.

Tying arrangements involve the forced purchase of two distinct products or services. When the tying product or service market is characterised by monopoly or market dominance, such arrangements can be defined as having the effect of restricting competition in the tied product or service market. Tying arrangements include pure bundling, where products are always sold as a set; technical tying, where products are technically integrated to achieve the intended effects; and mixed bundling, where rebates are offered for purchasing multiple products together.[37] In the context of self-preferencing within the digital economy, technical tying could possibly be problematic.

Google Android

In *Google Android*,[38] Google tied the Google Search app to Play Store, and Google Chrome to both the Play Store and Google Search app. Additionally, Google implemented Anti-fragmentation Agreements (AFA) related to its licensing, as well as portfolio-based revenue share payments.

The Commission found that Google holds a dominant position in the global smartphone licensing market and the global Android app store market (both excluding China), and that non-licensable smartphone OSs, such as Apple and BlackBerry exercised insufficient indirect constraint on Google's dominant position in the worldwide market (excluding China) for Android app stores.[39]

The Commission[40] found that Play Store and Google Search app are distinct products, and that Play Store, which is dominant in the global market (excluding China), cannot be obtained without the Google Search app.[41]

Both forms of tying provide significant competitive advantages and strengthen Google's dominant position in each national market for general search services. This practice builds entry barriers, stifles innovation, then directly and indirectly harms consumers, all without objective justification.[42]

The Commission noted that different forms of practices were aimed at maintaining and strengthening the dominant position in the general search services, and that they are complementary since they pursue an identical objective to maintain and strengthen revenue through search advertising. The Commission concluded that the practices constitute a single and continuous infringement, and fined Google almost €4.343 billion.[43]

The ECJ largely upheld the Commission's decision. The ECJ noted that tying occurs when a dominant undertaking conditions the sale of the tying products on the purchase of the tied product, and that exclusionary effects can arise not only in the tied product market but also in the tying product market, or in both simultaneously. A dominant undertaking in the tying product market, or in several markets including the tying market, can harm consumers by foreclosing markets related to the tied product market.[44]

The GC examined the four factors[45] regarding tying: (1) "the tying and tied products are two separate products"; (2) "the undertaking concerned is dominant in the market for the tying product"; (3) "the undertaking concerned does not give customers a choice to obtain the tying product without the tied product";

and (4) "the practice in question forecloses competition." The GC concluded that Google's conduct constituted four factors and they were not objectively justified, and fined Google almost €4.125 billion.[46] However, the GC took a prudent stance to interpret 'restriction of competition' as a 'capacity to restrict competition' like the Commission.[47] Additionally, the ECJ denied the competitive restraint of portfolio-based revenue share payments. The ECJ was negative against the interpretation of 'capacity to restrict competition' with As Efficient Competitor test.[48]

Google Android and Tying in the Digital Economy

Typically, market power is leveraged from the tying product market to the tied product market. The Chicago School's single monopoly profit theory argues that a dominant undertaking cannot gain monopoly profits in the tied product market, but in the tying product market.[49] However, in *Google Android*, it is notable that Google possesses market power not only in the tying product market but also in the tied product market. This suggests that a dominant digital platform undertaking exerts market power across a series of complementary and interdependent markets, commonly referred to as the digital ecosystem. In such circumstances, a dominant digital platform undertaking may engage in defensive tying to maintain and strengthen its market power in both the tying and tied product markets, thereby excluding competitors or preventing new market entrants. In *Google Android*, it can be said that single and continuous conduct, including tying, constitutes an infringement of Article 102 TFEU to regulate preferential treatment by a dominant digital platform undertaking. Moreover, the traditional competition law framework, as an ex-post approach, remains valid addressing anti-competitive conduct in digital ecosystem markets.[50]

In Japan, the Japan Fair Trade Commission (JFTC) also launched an investigation into tying practices of *Google Android* in October 2023. The JFTC claimed that Google licensed Google Play together with Google Search and Google Chrome, raising concerns that Google may have done so to exclude competitors or to restricted the business activities of its counterparties. Additionally, Google's revenue-sharing agreements for search result advertising services, conditioned on the non-installation of competing search applications, are suspected to exclude competing enterprises or restrict the business activities of its trading partners.[51]

The JFTC already expressed concern regarding Google's market position and a possible infringement of AMA. The JFTC has actively sought opinion and information from the third parties since 2022.[52] To efficiently collect information and effectively detect suspected violations of the AMA, the JFTC notified the stake holders concerning collecting information and comments in advance, and then disclosed the names of the enterprises and the summary of suspected conduct. The JFTC is expected to issue a cease-and-desist order against Google in 2025. This will be the first time the JFTC has issued such an order against GAFAM.

Preferential Treatment in Exclusive Dealing

It is possible to assess that a digital platform undertaking which also operates on the downstream market, engages in preferential treatment toward itself over its competitors. This raises the question of how competition law evaluates exclusive dealing practices by a dominant digital platform.

In *Google Search (AdSense),*[53] Google has operated an advertising intermediary platform called Google AdSense since 2003, providing an online search advertising intermediary service known as AdSense for Search (AFS). AFS allows website publishers to display advertisements related to users' search queries on their website.

The Commission[54] concluded that Google held a dominant position in both the online advertising market and the online advertising intermediary markets. Google's conduct, including (1) the Exclusivity Clause, (2) the Premium Placement and Minimum Google Ads Clause, and (3) the Authorizing Equivalent Ads Clause, as outlined in its Google Services Agreements (GSA), constituted a single and continuous infringement and violated Article 102 TFEU.[55]

The Commission concluded that GSA's exclusionary clause and Premium Placement and Minimum Google Ads Clause[56] and Authorising Equivalent Ads Clause[57] constitute a single and continuous infringement and fined Google almost €1.494 billion.

The GC noted that dominant undertakings have a special responsibility not to allow their behaviour to impair genuine, undistorted competition on the internal market.[58] To establish that conduct is abusive, the Commission is not necessarily required to demonstrate that the conduct actually produced anticompetitive effects. The Commission may find that there has been an infringement of Article 102 TFEU by establishing that, during the period in which the conduct in question was implemented, that conduct had the ability to restrict competition on the merit.[59] The GC concluded that GSA's foreclosure effect is not adequate[60] and overturned the Commission's Decision.

***Google AdSense* and Special Responsibility and Indispensability**

In *Google AdSense*, the Commission concluded that intermediated sales are indispensable for online advertising.[61] Moreover, dominant undertakings have a special responsibility.[62]

However, anticompetitive effects on the market are not sufficiently demonstrated in this case. In *Google AdSense*, the GC clarified that, while dominant undertakings have a special responsibility and intermediated sales are indispensable for online advertising, the Commission still needs to establish that, during the period in which the conduct in question was implemented, that conduct had the ability to restrict competition on the merit.[63]

In Japan, in the *Google AdTech* case,[64] Google restricted the technology, preventing Yahoo from conducting mobile syndication transactions. These transactions enable companies to distribute search advertisements and to share profits with website operators who provide advertising space. The JFTC noted that Google's actions were suspected of constituting private monopolisation (Article 3), unilateral refusal to deal (Paragraph 2 of the UTP Designation), and interference with a competitor's transactions (Paragraph 14 of the UTP Designation). Consequently, Google submitted a Commitment Plan to the JFTC and eased restricting the supply of technology necessary for mobile syndication transactions.

Legal Standard of Non-Price Exclusionary Conducts and Preferential Treatments

This chapter examines preferential treatments to its own products or services by dominant digital platform undertakings, particularly those with special responsibilities or offering indispensable products or services, under Article 102 TFEU. It focuses on the cases of *Google Shopping*, *Google Android*, and *Google AdSense*.

In the EU, most competition cases are administrative in nature, meaning market definition is not always a central issue, as the competition authorities have the ability to gather sufficient data and evidence.[65] However, in jurisdictions like the US where many antitrust cases are civil, the capacity to collect data and evidence is more limited, therefore, market definition is a significant point of contention. In the *US Google case*,[66] the relevant market is defined more narrowly than in the EU, focusing on the general search text ads market rather than the broader online search advertising and its intermediation market.

Once the market is defined, the Commission must prove the restriction of competition. In *Google Shopping*, self-preferencing involves discriminative practices, such as favouring Google's own products while demoting those of competitors.[67] Furthermore, according to the ECJ, it is not necessary to establish the indispensability of the service. However, exclusionary effects – typically foreclosure effects in downstream markets – must be demonstrated.

Self-preferencing represents a novel form of anticompetitive conduct. Regarding the extent of evidence required to demonstrate competitive harm, actual exclusionary effects are not required; it is sufficient to prove the potential for such effect.

In the context of tying, a dominant digital platform undertaking may hold market power not only in the market for tying products but also in the market for tied products. Regarding exclusive dealing, the Commission may find an infringement of Article 102 TFEU by demonstrating that the conduct had the ability to restrict competition on the merit. However, the GC appears to require proof of actual restriction of competition on the merit. Conversely, in *Google Shopping*, the ECJ emphasised that it is necessary to demonstrate – using methods beyond mere competition on the merits – that such conduct has either the actual or potential effect of restricting competition by excluding equally efficient competitors from the relevant market(s)[68] or by hindering their growth in those markets. Generally, the legal standard for establishing an infringement of Article 102 TFEU is nearly the same approach but the burden of proof is somewhat different.

In relation to exclusive dealing, it is considered that, in determining the anticompetitive effects, the focus should be on whether such effect has actually occurred, rather than merely the potential to restrict competition. This would require clear proof of anticompetitive effects in cases involving exclusive dealing.

A common feature of tying and exclusive dealing is that both practices are treated as a single and continuous conduct. This regulatory approach, which does not exist in the US or Japan, offers perspective on regulating the digital platform market that shapes the digital ecosystem. However, it may not be assessed as an integrated act unless a clear anticompetitive effect is identified.[69]

Conclusion

In the EU, where administrative cases are predominant, market definition typically poses no significant issues. However, in jurisdictions where civil lawsuits are more common, market definition in complex digital markets can be challenging due to the limited capacity of private parties to collect evidence. In civil litigation, there is a tendency to narrowly define the market and apply it to a form of presumed illegality.

Even under EU competition law, which actively regulates self-preferencing, the practice itself is not considered illegal by objective. Self-preferencing is regulated based on an effects-based approach. Regulating self-preferencing through ex-ante regulation targeting Big Tech companies is a logical step.

However, there are measures that can be taken through ex post regulation. In this chapter, the *Google Shopping* case clarifies the nature of self-preferencing in the context of competition law, which operates as an ex post regulation. While indispensability is not a mandatory requirement for self-preferencing in Google Shopping, it is clear that indispensability increases the likelihood of foreclosure effects in downstream markets.

Thus, the definition of self-preferencing remains unclear. However, actions by digital platform operators that give preferential treatment to their own services or products can be deemed illegal if they meet the traditional requirement for tying and exclusive dealing. In any case, the interpretation of such practices is often an extension of traditional rulings when a dominant digital IT operator engages in preferential treatment within the digital platform market.

The degree of proof required to establish exclusionary effects varies depending on the type of conduct. In particular, for exclusive dealing, providing anticompetitive effects seems to require demonstrating actual impact more than for other types of conduct. The fact that different types of conduct require different levels of proof, leading to inconsistencies in the criteria for determining illegality, can be seen as a potential issue for the future. Furthermore, after determining illegality, the approach to enforcement is also crucial in the digital sector.[70]

Notes

This work was supported by JSPS KAKENHI Grant Number JP23K01133.

1 Marc Wiggers, Robin Struijlaart, Joost Dibbits, *Digital Competition Law in Europe* (Kluwer Law International B.V. 2023), 5–6.

2 Michael G. Jacobides, Carmelo Cennamo, Annabelle Gawer, 'Towards a Theory of Ecosystem', *Strategic Management Journal,* 39 (8) (2018) 2255, 2256–2258.
3 Amelia Fletcher, 'Digital Competition Policy: Are Ecosystems Different?' (2020) OECD DAF/COMP/WD(2020)96, 2, 5-7; Michael G. Jacobides, Carmelo Cennamo, Annabelle Gawer, 'Externalities and Complementarities in Platforms and Ecosystems From Structural Solutions to Endogenous Failures' (2024), *Research Policy*, 53(1) Article 104906, 12.
4 Michael G. Jacobides, Martin Bruncko, Rene Lange, 'Regulating Big Tech in Europe' (2020) White Paper, 30–36
5 Michael G. Jacobides, Martin Bruncko, Rene Lange, 'Regulating Big Tech in Europe'.
6 Vertical integration, data-driven advantages, dominance, and access to private users may further strengthen dominance in the digital sector. See Lukas Solek, 'Concept of Dominance in the Digital Age' (2023) 44(5) 194–200.
7 Crémer et al., 'Fairness and Contestability in the Digital Markets Act' (2023) *Yale J. on Regul.,* 40 (forthcoming); Kohei Kawaguchi, Toshifumi Kuroda, Susumu Sato, 'Merger Analysis in the App Economy: An Empirical Model of Ad-Sponsored Media' (2021) HKUST CEP Working Paper No. 2021-03. See also Peter O'Loughlin, 'Default Power in Global Antitrust Enforcement' (2024) 45(4) 155–162.
8 Personalised Pricing refers to 'any practice of price discriminating final consumers based on their personal characteristics and conduct, resulting in prices being set as an increasing function of consumers' willingness to pay.' OECD, 'Personalised Pricing in the Digital Era' (2018) ¶17; CMA, 'Pricing Algorithm – Economic Working Paper on the Use of Algorithms to Facilitate Collusion and Personal Pricing' (2018) §7.2
9 In Japan, an example of a case where ranking manipulation because an issue is the *Tabelog* case. See *Tabelog, Tokyo High Court, Reiwa 4 nenn (Ne) dai 3422 gou songaibaishouseikyukousojiken* [the Appeal of Damage Claim in Case Reiwa 2nd year (Ne) No. 3422] (19 January 2024).
10 See Wiggers, Struijlaart, Dibbits (n 1 above) 26–27.
11 See Yuta Kittaka, Susumu Sato, 'Dual-Role Platforms and Self-Preferencing: Sequential Search Approach' (2022) 2-4, SSRN. https://ssrn.com/abstract=3736574
12 Yuta Kittaka, Susumu Sato, Yusuke Zennyo, 'Self-Preferencing by Platforms: A Literature Review' (2022) CPRC Discussion Paper Series, CPDP-89-2-E, 17–31. https://www.jftc.go.jp/cprc/reports/disucussionpapers/r4/index_files/CPDP-89-2-E-R.pdf
13 Allison Jones, Brenda Sufrin, Niamh Dunne, *EU Competition Law* (8th ed. Oxford University Press 2023) 546–556.
14 Wiggers, Struijlaart, Dibbits (n 1 above) 27.
15 Case T-612/17 Google and Alphabet v Commission (Google Shopping), ECLI: EU: T: 2021: 763.
16 Case AT.40462 Amazon Marketplace and Case AT.40703 Amazon Buy Box, Commission Decision of 20 Dec. 2022.
17 In Korea, Naver case (KFTC Decision No. 2021-027, 2018 Seogam 2521 (27 January 2021); Seoul High Court Judgment 2021Nu36129 (14 December 2022), Kakao Taxi case (KFTC Decision No. 2023-093, 2021Sigam0760 (13 June 2023), the Seoul High Court, pending) can be cited as prominent examples of self-preferencing.
18 Herbert Hovenkamp, 'Antitrust and Self-Preferencing' (2023) 38 (1) Antitrust 1, 5.
19 Jonathan Kanter, 'Assistant Attorney General Jonathan Kanter of the Antitrust Division Delivers Remarks at the Keystone Conference on Antitrust Regulation & the Political Economy' (2 March 2023).
20 There is a comparative study between the EU and the US. See Tânia Luísa Faria, 'Guilherme Neves Lima, Abuse of a Dominant Position in the Digital Economy in the EU and US' (2020) 41 (3) E.C.L.R. 144–151.
21 Digital Markets Act [2022] OJ L265/1.
22 Act on Promotion of Competition for Specified Smartphone Software [2024] Act No. 58 of 2024.

23 Case C-48/22 P Google LLC, Alphabet Inc., v Commission [2024] ECLI:EU:C:2024:726.
24 Google Search (Shopping) (Case AT.39740) [2017] Commission Decision of 27 June 2017 [2018] OJ C9/11.
25 Case T-612/17 Google LLC, Alphabet Inc., v Commission [2021] ECLI:EU:T:2021:763 para. 681.
26 Case T-612/17 Google LLC, Alphabet Inc., v Commission [2021], paras. 164–165.
27 Case T-612/17 Google LLC, Alphabet Inc., v Commission [2021], para. 224.
28 Case C-48/22 P Google LLC, Alphabet Inc., v Commission [2024] ECLI:EU:C:2024:726.
29 Case C-48/22 P Google LLC, Alphabet Inc., v Commission [2024], para. 87.
30 Case C-48/22 P Google LLC, Alphabet Inc., v Commission [2024], para. 163.
31 Case C-48/22 P Google LLC, Alphabet Inc., v Commission [2024], paras. 170–172.
32 Case C-48/22 P Google LLC, Alphabet Inc., v Commission [2024], para. 83.
33 Case C-48/22 P Google LLC, Alphabet Inc., v Commission [2024], para. 109.
34 Case C-48/22 P Google LLC, Alphabet Inc., v Commission [2024], para. 165.
35 Alison Jones, Brenda Sufrin, Niamh Dunne, *EU Competition Law* (Oxford University Press 2023) 547–548.
36 Alison Jones, Brenda Sufrin, Niamh Dunne, *EU Competition Law,* 552. Professor Dunne emphasizes the importance of fairness to make markets work better. Niamh Dunne, 'Fairness and the Challenge of Making Markets Work Better' (2021) 84(2) M.L.R. 230–264.
37 See Rhodri Thompson QC, Chritopher Brown, and Nicholas Gibson, 'Article 102' in David Bailey and Laura Elizabeth John (eds), *European Union Law of Competition* (Oxford University Press, 8th edn, 2018) 947.
38 Case T-604/18 Google LLC, Alphabet, Inc., v EC Commission [2022] OJ C 83/11.
39 Case T-604/18 Google LLC, Alphabet, Inc., v EC Commission [2022], para. 659.
40 Google Android (Case AT.40099) Commission Decision of 18.7.[2018]
41 Google Android (Case AT.40099), para. 754.
42 Google Android (Case AT.40099), para. 773.
43 Google Android (Case AT.40099), paras. 739, 1341.
44 Google Android (Case AT.40099), para. 283.
45 See T-201/04 Microsoft v Commission [2007] EU:T:2007:289, para. 869.
46 Google Android (n 38 above) para. 284.
47 Google Android (n 38 above), paras. 296, 299.
48 Google Android (n 38 above), paras. 795–797.
49 See Robert H. Bork, *The Antitrust Paradox* (Basic Books, 1978) 372–375.
50 The GC found that, with regard to user preference, 95% of users prefer Google's general search engine. However, Google's general search engine is pre-installed and set as the default setting web browser (para. 462). This pre-installation is likely to influence user behavior. See Bruce Wardhaugh, 'European Union: Anti-Competitive Practices-Judgement-Restrictive business Practices' (2022) 44(3) E.C.L.R. N51-N52.
51 JFTC, 'Press Release: The JFTC Opens an Investigation and Seeks Information and Comments from Third Parties Concerning the Suspected Violation of the Antimonopoly Act by Google LLC, etc.' (October 23, 20023), https://www.jftc.go.jp/file/231023EN.pdf
52 See JFTC, 'Active Promotion of Competition Policy in Response to Changes in Digitalization and Social Economy' (16 June 2022) (in Japanese).
53 Case T-334/19 Google LLC, Alphabet Inc., v European Commission (Google AdSense) [2024] ECLI:EU:T:2024:634.
54 Case AT.40411 Google Search (AdSense) [2020] OJ C 369/6.
55 Case AT.40411 Google Search (AdSense) [2020], paras. 239, 286.
56 This clause allows users to make a reservation in a prominent space.
57 This clause requires Google's consent to change display competing search advertisement.
58 Google AdSense (n 55 above) paras. 104–105.
59 Google AdSense (n 55 above), para. 108.

60 The Commission considered cumulative period. However, most of GSA lasts only for 2–3 years or renewed or extended.

61 Google AdSense (n 55 above) para. 308.

62 Google AdSense (n 55 above), para. 104.

63 Google AdSense (n 55 above), para. 108.

64 JFTC, 'Press Release: Approval of the Commitment Plan submitted by Google LLC' (22 April 2024), https://www.jftc.go.jp/en/pressreleases/yearly-2024/April/240422.html

65 See Daniel Mandrescu, 'The Commission Notice on the Definition of the Relevant Market and Multi-sided Digital Platforms-Small but Important Steps Forward' 45(8) E.C.L.R. (2024) 45(8) 359-370.

66 United States et al. v. Google LLC, No. 1:20-cv-03010-APM (D.D.C. 2024).

67 There is a study examining discrimination by digital platforms. Wolf Sauter, Hans Vedder, 'Anti-competitive Discrimination by Digital Platforms', 44(3) E.C.L.R. (2023) 88–97.

68 There is a criticism that it is hard to imagine a company as efficient as Big Tech companies, and thus out an AEC test is deeply problematic in digital markets. Sauter and Vedder (n 67 above) 96.

69 See e.g., Google AdSense (n 55 above).

70 See e.g., United States et al. v. Google LLC, No. 1:20-cv-03010-APM (D.D.C. 2024). See also Thomas Hoehn, Justin Menezes, Alison Young, 'Big Tech Remedies' (2023) 44(2) E.C.L.R. 47–60.

3 Fair Competition and Appropriate Use of Data and Algorithms in the Digital Platform Business-Case Studies and Policy Approaches in Japan

Kentaro Hirayama

Introduction

Digital platforms bring many benefits to people's lives and the economy, such as dramatically increasing access to domestic and foreign markets by small and medium-sized enterprises (SMEs) and start-ups, and improving consumer benefits. However, digital platforms are prone to monopolisation and oligopoly through network effects and economies of scale. Businesses that are forced to rely on digital platforms for transactions have raised concerns about various transactional issues.

In Japan, in addition to Big Tech companies such as GAFA (Google, Amazon, Facebook, and Apple), there are also domestic digital platforms such as Yahoo Japan and LINE, which had tens of millions of users and developed their business mainly in Japan and recently merged into a single entity. Digital platform businesses in Japan have developed uniquely in a competitive landscape that differs from that of Europe and the US.

Under such unique circumstances in Japan, the fairness of the use of data by algorithms and the refusal to access user data by digital platforms have been repeatedly examined from the perspective of competition law through investigations by the Japan Fair Trade Commission (JFTC) and civil litigation. Moreover, doubts have recently been expressed about the effectiveness of an ex post investigation by the JFTC into anti-competitive conduct. New legislation is therefore rapidly being developed to regulate conduct that threatens fair competition ex ante through dialogue between government and business.

This chapter introduces cases in Japan where the fairness of using user data and other data using algorithms and denying access to user data have been analysed from the perspective of competition law. This chapter then introduces newly introduced ex ante regulations

Regulation of Digital Platform Businesses by the JFTC

In Japan, the JFTC has had exclusive authority to apply the Antimonopoly Act and take administrative action against companies for more than 75 years since 1947. Since the early 2010s, the JFTC has conducted various examinations and regulations

DOI: 10.4324/9781003489542-3

against unfair trade practices, corporate acquisitions, and business alliances by digital platform businesses to ensure the proper use of data and algorithms. This section introduces representative examples of examinations and regulations by the JFTC and explains how the JFTC analysed the impact of the use of data and algorithms on fair competition.

Business Cooperation between Yahoo Japan and Google

This case involved business cooperation between Yahoo Japan and Google Inc. Yahoo Japan, a large Japanese digital platform, would receive technology support from Google Inc. for its search engine and search-linked advertising system. The two companies discussed the matter with the JFTC to ensure it does not violate Japan's Antimonopoly Act. The JFTC concluded that the provision of this technology was not a problem under the Antimonopoly Act.[1]

Yahoo Japan did not have a search engine or advertising system for use on its websites, and had thus been provided with them by Yahoo Inc. of the United States until then. However, as Yahoo Japan could no longer continue to receive the search engine and advertising system from Yahoo Inc. of the US, it decided to select Google's search engine and advertising system as a new search engine and advertising system, judging it to be the most suitable for its company.

Yahoo Japan and Google explained to the JFTC that, even after implementing this business alliance, they would continue operating their Internet search services and search-linked advertising business independently and would maintain a competitive relationship by keeping advertisers' bidding prices and other information separate.

Specifically, Yahoo Japan explained to the JFTC that, since Yahoo Japan independently analyses the search keywords entered by users and then transmits the search keywords to Google's search engine, even if the exact search keywords are used for searches on the websites of Yahoo Japan and Google, the search data may differ between searches conducted via Yahoo Japan's website and those conducted directly from Google's website. Yahoo Japan further elaborated that if the search data entered into the search engine is different, the search results displayed on the websites of Yahoo and Google will be different. Furthermore, Yahoo Japan explained to the JFTC that it adds unique information when displaying search results.

Based on the above explanations, the JFTC examined the proposed business alliance and concluded in 2010 that (i) Yahoo Japan, as a user of search engines and advertising systems, selects Google's search engine because it is the most suitable for its use, and (ii) even after the implementation of this business alliance, competition between Yahoo Japan and Google concerning Internet search services and search-linked advertising business will continue, and therefore this will not immediately become an issue under the antimonopoly Act.

It is clear from the above that the JFTC found this business alliance to be acceptable based on the above explanation by Yahoo Japan and Google, by carefully conducting impact on competition arising from the use of data. However, the JFTC also took into account that (i) as a result of this business alliance, approximately

90% of the technology for search engines and advertising systems in Japan will belong to Google, and (ii) if this business alliance is not implemented as explained by Yahoo and Google, it will potentially have a significant impact on the market of Internet search services and search-linked advertising, and thus the JFTC mentioned that substantive impact may occur if the above (ii) would happen.

However, the business alliance with Yahoo Japan and Google was subsequently transformed into something different from the consultation content described above. More specifically, Google demanded that Yahoo Japan not serve search-linked advertisements using Google's technology to smartphone-oriented websites in 2014, so Yahoo has not been able to distribute search-linked advertisements thereafter. When the JFTC became aware of this, it launched an investigation against Google in 2022, which resulted in a settlement with the JFTC in 2024, as Google offered to take corrective measures. The JFTC concluded its investigation without issuing a cease-and-desist order, which is an administrative penalty.[2]

This case is a pioneering and essential example of a debate on the fairness of handling user data and other data at a time when concerns about digital platforms from a competition law perspective were not as strong as they are today. In addition, the fact that the JFTC was unable to discover the fact for a long time until recently that the content of this business alliance changed suggests that the JFTC's investigative capacity was insufficient.

The Merger between Yahoo Japan and LINE Corporation

This case involves the merger between a dominant platform in the QR code payment sector and the Social Networking Service (SNS) sector. Yahoo Japan (parent company Z Holdings), a large Japanese digital platform with a strong position in search services and payment services, merged with LINE Corporation, a large digital platform with a large social networking service with the majority of Japanese nationals registered as users. Yahoo Japan and LINE submitted a mandatory notification to the JFTC in 2019 before closing the merger. The JFTC approved the case in 2020, and the business integration was completed in 2021.[3]

The JFTC's investigation focused on smartphone payment services using Quick Response (QR) codes, in which Yahoo Japan and LINE competed. Yahoo Japan's PayPay was in the lead with a 55% market share; meanwhile, a competing service by LINE had a 5% share but a 25% market share before LINE stopped its promotional campaign in early 2019.

The JFTC was concerned that LINE's market share in the QR code payment market could increase again due to the broad user base of LINE's messaging application, which is used by two-thirds of the population in Japan. However, the JFTC found it challenging to predict future trends as the overall situation in the code payment market is in flux.

Interestingly, although the JFTC could not find that the business combination could substantially restrict competition, it demonstrated its willingness to require parties to a business combination to take monitoring and other measures to address competition concerns. More specifically, during its investigation, the JFTC discovered that Yahoo Japan and LINE had imposed exclusive conditions on some shops not to adopt payment systems competing with those of the two companies. Yahoo Japan and LINE voluntarily offered a package of remedial measures which consisted of removal of these exclusive clauses from the agreement, commitment not to impose such conditions for three years, and annual reporting to the JFTC on the status of the implementation of these measures for three years. Subject to these measures being observed, the JFTC approved the merger.

This case was noteworthy because the JFTC was willing to investigate a merger in which the fairness of handling user data, such as the usage history of social networking services (SNS) and QR code payment services, was an important issue. However, the fact that the JFTC hesitated to block the business integration case showed that the JFTC's investigative capacity was limited. It is also questionable whether the measures taken by Yahoo Japan and LINE to report to the JFTC for three years were sufficient to resolve concerns that there would be a negative impact on competition.

Formal Investigation against Airbnb Japan

This case involves an investigation by the JFTC against Airbnb Japan and its parent company for alleged breaches of the prohibition of transactions with exclusive conditions and restriction to competitors' access to data. Airbnb's business partners are reservation management companies commissioned by room owners (hosts) to post information on the intermediary platform's website and manage reservations for room owners.

The JFTC has found that Airbnb Japan's contract with the reservation management service providers restricts them, when posting information on available rooms on Airbnb Japan's website using the Application Programming Interface (API), from posting information on the same rooms on other intermediary platforms. For the operators of accommodation platforms competing with Airbnb Japan, Airbnb Japan's act of enclosing data, such as information on room vacancies, would mean that competitors would be denied access to data on available rooms which is virtually essential for their business. Open access to such data appears necessary to maintain a fair competition and contestable market in this industry.

The JFTC launched an investigation into Airbnb Japan because it was concerned that the abovementioned restriction would lead to the exclusion of operators of other intermediary platforms. Subsequently, Airbnb Japan offered the JFTC to promptly take measures to waive its right to apply the above provisions to the contracts in question with the counterparty mentioned above. After examining the content of the offer, the JFTC concluded its examination of the case in 2018 without any administrative sanctions, as it considered that the measures would resolve the potential competition law problem.[4]

Concerning this case, it should be noted that, at the time, the provision of accommodation services by house owners was strictly restricted in Japan by the Hotel Business Law, and the situation of competition between accommodation services in the form of providing hotel rooms and accommodation services utilising houses appears to have been very different. This should have affected the definition of a relevant market and thus also affected the calculation of Airbnb's market share if the fact had been carefully considered. In addition, while the JFTC's investigation was ongoing, a new law, the Residential Accommodation Business Law, came into force in 2018, lifting the ban on providing accommodation services using houses. Therefore, the industry for accommodation services using residences was amid a dynamic and comprehensive change in the competitive situation. These circumstances might have made it more complex and challenging for the JFTC to assess the anti-competitive effects of Airbnb's exclusionary agreements on future competition between Airbnb and its competitors.

According to an article by the JFTC official who was in charge of investigating this case,[5] when Airbnb Japan submitted its corrective action proposal, the JFTC had not concluded whether Airbnb Japan's conduct constituted a breach of the Antimonopoly Act. However, according to this explanatory article, the JFTC concluded that the suspicion of an antimonopoly act violation would be resolved if Airbnb Japan implemented the corrective measures and, on the assumption that the corrective measures would be implemented promptly, announced that it would terminate its examination once the implementation of the corrective measures was confirmed. According to this explanatory article, the JFTC decided that, with the environment of competition rapidly changing with the implementation of the Residential Accommodation Business Law, the emergence of network effects, which is one of the characteristics of the platform business, could have had a more significant negative impact on competition, and therefore made it a priority to improve the competitive environment at an early stage, and the investigation was concluded with the priority of improving the competitive environment as soon as possible.

In this case, it seems that the JFTC fully understood that competition over digital platforms is intense and fluid. This was why the JFTC proceeded with the investigation expeditiously; we can understand that concluding the investigation early before the adverse effects on competition could become substantive was considered important. On the other hand, the JFTC's emphasis on speed appears to have led it to hastily conclude its investigation even though it had not yet concluded issues such as the scope of the relevant market and effects on competition, which are essential for analysing cases under the Antimonopoly Act.

While this case is an important example for understanding the need for speedy regulation of digital platforms and the specific methods of such regulation, it is regrettable that, probably due to the emphasis on speedy examination, the JFTC did not make specific suggestions or a framework for assessment of future digital platform cases. Continued efforts by the JFTC to address this issue are highly appreciated.

Regulation of Digital Platform Businesses through Civil Litigation

As explained above, the JFTC has investigated digital platform businesses in Japan. In addition, there have been other cases where the judicial courts have provided interpretations of the Antimonopoly Act through civil lawsuits brought by counterparties to digital platforms.

In recent years, there has been a case in which a restaurant has filed lawsuits against 'Tabe-log'.[6] This company operates a nationwide business in Japan that introduces restaurants on its website and gives each restaurant a score out of five on web pages allocated to respective restaurants, alleging that their scores have been rapidly reduced without prior notice. In the litigation, a restaurant filed a lawsuit against Tabe-log. The case was unique in that Tabe-log provided the Tokyo High Court with a detailed explanation of the content of the algorithm, including the factors taken into account by the algorithm used to calculate the score, although third parties cannot inspect the documents as the explanatory notes of the algorithm are redacted for third parties' inspection. The Tokyo High court used this as a basis for its decision.

The case was also critical in that a decision made clear that it is difficult for the plaintiff (restaurant) to prove illegality. The Tokyo District Court partially accepted the plaintiff's (restaurant) claim for damages because Tabe-log had abused its dominant position, but a subsequent decision by the Tokyo High Court overturned the District Court's decision and ruled in favour of the defendant, (Tabe-log), that there was no abuse of a dominant position or other violation of antitrust law, resulting in the defendant's reverse victory in the case.

According to the Tokyo High Court decision, the scores of restaurants on Tabe-log were calculated by an algorithm based on the scores given by contributors and by taking into account various factors based on the idea that contributors with more experience in eating out would have a greater degree of influence in determining the score of the restaurants. In 2019, Tabe-log decided that (i) the algorithm needed to be corrected due to the discrepancy between the ratings of each restaurant on the Tabe-log website and the perceptions of consumers on the same restaurants, and (ii) the algorithm also needed to be adjusted to a better deal with fraudulent techniques to manipulate the scores of restaurants.

The Tokyo High Court then acknowledged that the number of visitors to the restaurants operated by the plaintiff from the Tabe-log website decreased after each of the restaurants operated by the plaintiff had experienced a drop in their respective scores, but noted that it was not clear to what extent the number of visitors had decreased significantly compared to competing restaurants where the scores had not dropped. The judgment also stated that the algorithm change did not go so far as to suppress the autonomy of the plaintiffs, that the algorithm was scheduled to be reviewed regularly, and that changes in scores were publicly announced on the Tabe-log website. On these grounds, the Tokyo High Court held that Tabe-log's conduct of changing the algorithm did not amount to its abuse of a superior position and did not constitute any other violation of antitrust law (discriminatory treatment).

This decision is a good example that the court can confirm that it will not hesitate to hear technical issues such as algorithms and that discussing the antitrust law violations of the use of algorithms and data handling in court is practicable. However, the decision also made clear that, when examining a case from the perspective of abuse of a superior position in antitrust law, the critical factors to be considered by the court in finding illegality include (i) whether the conduct under consideration was of such intensity that it could be said to have reached the point of suppressing the autonomy of the restaurant, and (ii) the extent to which the number of visitors to the restaurant was significantly declined in comparison with competing restaurants whose rating were unchanged. These are facts that JFTC had not indicated in previous administrative actions (cease-and-desist orders) or guidelines, and in particular, the latter fact (ii) could give rise to a situation where the plaintiff is required to investigate and argue in court the number of customers who visited the competing restaurant, which is considered a trade secret, but which is impossible to prove in practice. To explain this differently, it appears that the Tokyo High Court required the plaintiff to prove a fact it could not demonstrate in practice.

As far as I was aware from publicly available information, there are still only a few examples of attempts to regulate digital platform businesses through civil litigation. It is difficult to anticipate that the use of court proceedings will immediately and rapidly expand in Japan since the possibility of retaliation, such as termination of business relations, must be assumed in practice and since methods for collecting evidence held by the opposing party in litigation proceedings are extremely limited. That said, the number of court cases is likely to gradually increase as people become more aware of what constitutes a breach of the Antimonopoly Act through media coverage of the JFTC's investigations into digital platforms. The launch of a number of investigations into digital platforms by the JFTC and widespread media coverage of the investigations will likely help the Japanese public and Japanese lawyers to have a better understanding of what plaintiffs should argue in civil proceedings, and thereby help them to make decisions to bring a civil action easier than at present.

Introduction of Co-regulation Scheme – the DPF Transparency and Fairness Act

Introduction

In response to the concerns that could arise from the oligopolisation of digital platforms, as explained at the beginning of this chapter, the Act on Improvement of Transparency and Fairness in Trading on Specified Digital Platforms (DPF Transparency and Fairness Act) was passed by the Diet and came into effect in 2021.[7] Unlike the antitrust law, this Act is administered by the Japanese Ministry of Economy, Trade and Industry (METI).

The DPF Transparency and Fairness Act aims to improve transparency and fairness between digital platforms and their users (Transacting Party) through disclosing information on transaction terms and conditions and developing voluntary procedures and systems by digital platform providers.

The basic principle is that improvements should be made voluntarily and that the government's involvement and regulation should be kept to the minimum necessary (Article 3 of the Act). As Table 3.1 shows below, the Act then designates the providers of digital platform services (Designated Platforms) and imposes certain obligations on the designated operators.

Table 3.1 List of the Designated Platforms

Online Shopping Mall	*App Store*	*Digital Ads*
Amazon Japan	Alphabet (Google)	Alphabet (Google)
Rakuten (Japanese domestic platform)	Apple/iTunes	Meta (Facebook)
LINE-Yahoo (Japanese domestic platform)		LINE-Yahoo (Japanese domestic platform)

Source: Author.

The Designated Platforms in the online shopping mall and app store business were designated in 2021, followed by the designation of the Designated Platforms in digital advertising business in 2022.

Obligations of the Designated Platform

The obligations imposed on the Designated Platform include the following (Articles 4, 5, 7, and 9):

- Obligation to disclose information, such as prior disclosure of transaction terms and conditions and notification at certain conducts, such as when changing transaction terms and conditions,
- Obligation to establish voluntary procedures and systems for handling complaints and disputes,
- Obligation to submit a report with a self-evaluation of measures implemented.

The DPF Transparency and Fairness Act is positioned as a complement to antitrust law, as it seeks to prevent violations of antitrust law. The Act includes a provision allowing the METI to request that the JFTC take measures such as administrative cease-and-desist orders (Article 13).

Consideration of Consumers' Interest through Regulation on the Use of Algorithm

The DPF Transparency and Fairness Act regulates the business relationship between digital platforms and the Transacting Party to a certain degree. Although some fear that protecting the Transacting Party may harm consumers' interests, the DPF Transparency and Fairness Act contains provisions that consider consumer interests and other factors and consumer interests are considered in the enforcement of the DPF Transparency and Fairness Act.

For example, the METI considers it a precondition for businesses of the Designated Platform that algorithms may be used to determine the ranking and search results of products displayed on the platform's website. Thus, the METI has requested the Designated Platform to disclose the critical considerations used by the algorithm to determine the ranking results. Interestingly, the DPF Transparency and Fairness Act requires that the disclosure must be made not only to the Transacting Party but also to consumers (Article 5(2)(i)(c) and (ii)(a)).

Since the order in which products are displayed significantly impacts consumers' purchasing behaviour, Transacting Parties' business may be unduly harmed if the order in which products are displayed is arbitrarily manipulated by the use of algorithms by the Designated Platforms. In other words, unfair use of algorithms by the Designated Platform is therefore likely to concurrently harm the interests of Transacting Parties and consumers. This is why the Act requires the Designated Platform to disclose information concerning algorithms, and by requiring the disclosure, the DPF Transparency and Fairness Act expects that consumers' reasonable interests and those of Transacting Parties would be effectively protected.

'Agile Governance' Approach under Co-regulation Scheme

The DPF Transparency and Fairness Act is unique in that it encourages the improvement of the operation of digital platforms through monitoring by the administration and relevant parties.

The METI reviews the transparency and fairness of digital platform operation based on the submitted annual reports, while also listening to the opinions of users, professors, and lawyers. This process of 'monitoring and review' encourages the sharing of issues and mutual understanding between the parties concerned and leads to improved transparency and fairness of the digital platform. Such a mechanism incorporates the so-called 'co-regulation' concept. The METI expects the Designated Platform to take a flexible stance to make improvements when issues are identified, which it calls 'Agile Governance'.

More specifically, in December 2021, the Monitoring Meeting on Transparency and Fairness of Digital Platforms (Monitoring Meeting) was established, and experts from various fields including competition law, information law and economics were appointed as members. Since then, the Monitoring Meeting has been discussing various issues, such as app store fees and billing methods, concerns about the company's preferential treatment regarding the display ranking of products, account suspension, and handling of returns and refunds. Based on these discussions, the evaluation results by METI were published annually in December 2022 and February 2024 so far.[8]

The DPF Transparency and Fairness Act has had three positive effects on the trading environment.

First, the DPF Transparency and Fairness Act has been implemented, and the Designated Platforms have been working on various improvements including the disclosure of easy-to-understand information in the Japanese language, and on the development of a system for complaint handling. In the questionnaire survey results, many Transacting Parties indicated that the handling of complaints has improved.

The second point is the effective review of individual disputes. In cases where a potential breach of the DPF Transparency and Fairness Act exists, the Designated Platform took voluntary restoration measures and measures to prevent recurrence and thereby fair transactions have been restored.

The third point is the effectiveness of the Ministerial Assessment. The Ministerial Evaluation includes the expected direction of action (improvements) for the Designated Platform. Under the Transparency Act, Designated Platforms must improve their operations based on the ministerial evaluation and are expected to work voluntarily and proactively. Unfortunately, however, some violations of the Transparency Act continue, so the METI has issued guidance and made public in 2024 that Amazon Japan and Apple did not adequately disclose changes in contract terms and conditions to the Transacting Party, among other things, requiring them to correct the situation.

Proactive enforcement of the DPF Transparency and Fairness Act by METI is important to meet the expectations of the Transacting Party and the public that digital platforms operate without a loss of fairness. The abovementioned announcements by METI in 2024 are extremely noteworthy as they suggest that METI is willing to actively enforce the DPF Transparency and Fairness Act in the future.

Introduction of Ex Ante Regulation – Smartphone Software Competition Promotion Act

Introduction

As explained, the DPF Transparency and Fairness Act has significantly improved transparency and fairness of transactions through dialogues between Designated DPFs, the METI, and the Monitoring Meeting members. Meanwhile, the DPF Transparency and Fairness Act does not legally obligate or order Designated DPFs to adopt specific transaction conditions or conduct with specific content but merely encourages them to strive for improvement. Trading partners of Designated DPFs and consumers have, therefore, criticised the Act for failing to effectively regulate digital platforms.

Amid these discussions, a new law, the Smartphone Software Competition Promotion Act, was passed by Parliament in 2024 to address such criticisms and will enter into force at the end of 2025.[9] The Act focuses on smartphones, which are fundamental to people's lives, and also aims to promote competition in the software that is particularly necessary for the use of smartphones. The digital platforms to be regulated will be formally designated soon, using business size figures as a standard. Apple and Google are believed to be designated as regulated platforms.

Ex Ante Regulation under Potential Co-regulation Approach

The Smartphone Software Competition Promotion Act, like the Digital Market Act (DMA) enforced by the European Commission, legally imposes specific transaction conditions and conduct on large digital platforms that are designated as regulated. However, unlike the DMA, which almost comprehensively regulates the various services that constitute the digital platform ecosystem, the Smartphone Software Competition Promotion Act focuses only on smartphones. This Act does not comprehensively regulate transaction terms concerning various services provided by digital platforms.

The Smartphone Software Competition Promotion Act lists the following conduct as prohibited conduct or obligations for designated digital platforms, and we can understand from this list that the fair use of data is one of the focuses of this regulation.

- Prohibited conducts
    - Prohibition of improper use of acquired data (Article 5)
    - Prohibition of unfair treatment of app providers (Article 6)
    - Prohibition of interference with the provision of other app stores (Article 7)
    - Prohibition of interference with the use of mobile OS functions (Article 7)
    - Prohibition of interference with the use of other billing systems (Article 8)
    - Prohibition of restrictions on setting "outlink" and steering (Article 8)
    - Prohibition of interference with the use of other browser engines (Article 8)
    - Prohibition of forcing users to use their social login services (Article 8)
    - Prohibition of self-preferencing in displaying search results (Article 9)
- Obligations
    - Disclosure of the terms of use of acquired data (Article 10)
    - Transfer of acquired data to users (Article 11)
    - Measures to change default settings and display selection screens (Article 12)
    - Consent to additional installation of software (Article 12)
    - Disclosure of specification changes and others (Article 13)

The DMA provides a framework for co-regulation in which the Commission and digital platforms can work through dialogue on the specific measures to be taken for many of the obligations to be complied with by the digital platforms to be regulated. In Japan, as already explained, METI has introduced a co-regulatory framework in the Digital Platform Transparency Act and has achieved results, but it is not yet made clear how the co-regulatory framework will be used to enforce the Smartphone Software Competition Promotion Act.

Consideration of Privacy and Fairness

In the EU, digital platforms have been criticised by counterparties, consumer groups and others for insufficient efforts by regulated digital platforms to comply with their obligations under the DMA, and the Commission has launched investigations into alleged violations of the DMA against Alphabet, Apple, and Meta. If the DMA ultimately finds a violation of the DMA, in that case it will order the violating digital platforms to take corrective measures and levy administrative monetary penalties. For cumulative violations, it will also take measures such as divestiture.

Meanwhile, in Japan, the Smartphone Software Competition Promotion Act states that the Act will take into account the need to ensure privacy and the unfairness of conduct when finding a violation of the prohibition, which makes the Act not clear enough for operators and courts. Therefore, the JFTC may not be able to quickly identify violations of the Act and such a situation may undermine the effectiveness of the enforcement of the Act. In addition, the Act only orders violators to pay administrative monetary penalties for a limited number of types of conduct that can be categorically assumed to result in unduly large sales and excessive profits, which implies the JFTC's reluctance to impose significant monetary penalties on violators.

Potential for Overlapping Regulations by the METI and the JFTC

As already explained, the METI is in charge of enforcing the DPF Transparency and Fairness Act, and efforts are underway to make transaction conditions transparent and fair in the online shopping sector, smartphone software sector, and digital advertising sector. However, the Smartphone Software Competition Promotion Act, for which the JFTC will be in charge of enforcing, will introduce this new ex-ante regulation in the smartphone software sector, which could lead to a state of double regulation by two government agencies in the same sector.

It is understood that these two government agencies are discussing how their roles in future digital platform regulation will be allocated and aligned, and such discussions are necessary to avoid the unnecessary and unreasonable complexity of digital platform regulation.

Concluding Remarks

This chapter introduced the development of regulations of digital platforms in Japan over the past 15 years using the Antimonopoly Act by the JFTC and the courts, and then explained the current situation regarding recent attempts to regulate digital platforms using ex ante regulation approaches.

In the regulation of digital platforms in Japan, as in Europe and elsewhere, the focus has often been on the fairness of collection and use of data such as user data, and when discussing the use of data, the fairness of the use of algorithms has also been actively discussed.

New legislations in Japan have unique aspects that differ from legislations in Europe. The question of whether the new Japanese ex ante regulations are appropriate for the regulation of digital platforms in Japan should continue to be carefully monitored, considering the unique competitive landscape in Japan, where large domestic digital platforms such as the recently merged LINE-Yahoo still hold a significant position.

It is important, from this perspective, to continue to closely monitor whether or not digital platform regulation in Japan is the appropriate and the proportionate way to regulate digital platforms.

Notes

1 The Japan Fair Trade Commission, 'Yahoo Japan's Use of Technological Service Such as Search Engine Provided by Google (Tentative translation)', 2 December 2010, https://warp.ndl.go.jp/info:ndljp/pid/2922746/www.jftc.go.jp/en/pressreleases/archives/individual-000002.html

2 The Japan Fair Trade Commission, 'Approval of the Commitment Plan Submitted by Google LLC', 22 April 2024, https://www.jftc.go.jp/en/pressreleases/yearly-2024/April/240422.html

3 The Japan Fair Trade Commission, 'The JFTC Reviewed the Proposed Managerial Integration of Z Holdings Corporation and LINE Corporation (Tentative Translation)', 4 August 2020, https://www.jftc.go.jp/en/pressreleases/yearly-2020/August/200804.html

4 The Japan Fair Trade Commission, 'Closing the Investigation on the Suspected Violation of the Antimonopoly Act by Airbnb Ireland UC and Airbnb Japan K.K.', 10 October 2018, https://www.jftc.go.jp/en/pressreleases/yearly-2018/October/181010.html

5 Mr Osamu Igarashi and Mr Daiki Ikeda, 'Regarding a Resolution of Alleged Antitrust Violations against Airbnb Ireland U.C. and Airbnb Japan K.K.', (in Japanese), Kosei Torihiki, vol. 820, The Fair Trade Institute, 2019, pp. 84-88

6 *Hanryumura* v. *Kakaku.com*, Tokyo District Court Judgment of 16 June 2022, Case Reiwa 2 (Wa) No. 12735 and Tokyo High Cout Judgment of 19 January 2024, Case Reiwa 4(Ne) No. 3422

7 For the outline of the Act, please see The Ministry of Economy, Trade and Industry of Japan, 'Digital Platforms', https://www.meti.go.jp/english/policy/mono_info_service/information_economy/digital_platforms/index.html

8 The Ministry of Economy, Trade and Industry of Japan, 'Evaluation on Transparency and Fairness of Specified Digital Platforms Compiled' 22 December 2022, https://www.meti.go.jp/english/press/2022/1222_003.html and 2 February, 2024, https://www.meti.go.jp/english/press/2024/0202_002.html

9 The Japan Fair Trade Commission, 'Regarding the passage of the Act on Promotion of Competition for Specified Smartphone Software', 12 June 2024, https://www.jftc.go.jp/en/pressreleases/yearly-2024/June/240612.html

4 Cloud Computing and Competition Law

Shuya Hayashi and Kun-lin Wu

Introduction: What Is Cloud Computing?

In 2023, one of the most prominent M&A cases was Microsoft's proposed merger of Activision Blizzard,[1] which was notified to competition authorities in various countries for approval. In contrast to the early approvals granted by most of the competition authorities, including European Commission (EU), State Administration for Market Regulation (China), and Japan Fair Trade Commission (Japan), Competition and Markets Authority (UK) and Federal Trade Commission (US) have raised concerns over the impact of the merger on competition in the cloud gaming market,[2] as is estimated to keep thriving in the 2020s. Cloud gaming provides players with the ability to 'stream' games from cloud gaming servers to their own devices without the need for downloads and installations. This is enabled thanks to the cloud computing concept and related technologies, which is the main topic of this chapter.

Cloud computing lays a competition foundation for most digital services in the Internet economy. It provides businesses, including gaming companies, with access to necessary infrastructure, platform, or software 'as a service'. According to the US National Institute of Standards and Technology's definition,

> cloud computing is a model for enabling ubiquitous, convenient, on-demand network access to a shared pool of configurable computing resources (e.g., networks, servers, storage, applications, and services) that can be rapidly provisioned and released with minimal management effort or service provider interaction.[3]

In short terms, cloud computing refers to a service that provides on-demand availability of computing resources as services over the Internet. Traditionally, businesses need to arrange, deploy, and manage computing resources on premises by themselves. However, with the rise of cloud computing, businesses increasingly tend to embrace cloud services provided by third-party cloud service providers (CSPs) rather than deploying their own on-premise servers and running their software thereon, given the low running costs, flexibility, and ready access to advanced IT solutions. CSPs thus play a crucial role in the digital sector, and how they may enhance or distort competition therein deserves more attention.

DOI: 10.4324/9781003489542-4

In fact, cloud services have been recently targeted by competition authorities around the world as there are competition concerns including high market concentration and controversial practices adopted by dominant cloud providers.[4] Yet, it should be noted that competition over cloud services should be evaluated not only in terms of relevant markets on a case-by-case basis, but also from the perspective of ecosystem, which may encompass multiple types of cloud services and even non-cloud ones.[5] Indeed, some CSPs achieved their current market position arguably due to their customer's pre-existing use of the CSP's software products and services.[6] Moreover, whether the current high market concentration in the cloud services market, as indicated in all market studies mentioned in the subsequent paragraphs, stems from structural factors or not is also an important issue in determining the necessity, proportionality and effectiveness of the intervention of competition law.

In view of the importance of cloud services in the digital sector, this chapter thus puts its emphasis on competition issues related to cloud computing. Firstly, it gives an overview of the economic characteristics of cloud services, which convincingly explain the reason for high market concentration in the cloud services market. Secondly, it reviews recent market studies relating to cloud services to explore the consensus among competition authorities. Thirdly, instead of analysing the potential application of traditional competition law in the cloud services market, which has been extensively and thoroughly analysed in the market studies, it focuses on the recent EU legislation to understand the trend of regulating the cloud services market with ex ante and sector-specific regulations, and points out potential issues expected to arise following the introduction of such regulations. Finally, the last section concludes this chapter with a summary of the main findings and an outlook.

Economic Characteristics of Cloud Services: An Economic Perspective

Generally, cloud services are divided into three categories in accordance with their service models: infrastructure as a service (IaaS), platform as a service (PaaS), and software as a service (SaaS). As the names imply, they represent different service models.[7]

First, in the IaaS service model, CSPs offer their customers computing resources for processing workloads and storing data through the Internet. These computing resources, known as 'infrastructure', are in the form of servers and networking equipment owned and managed by the CSPs. Customers do not manage or control these underlying cloud infrastructures, but have control over the operating systems, databases and applications deployed by themselves.

Next, in the PaaS service model, CSPs provide access to a virtual development and deployment environment, understood as 'platform', over the Internet for their customers to develop, test, deploy, and run applications. These include application development computing platforms and pre-built application components and tools which customers can use to build and manage full applications therein. In this model, CSPs are responsible for managing the underlying cloud infrastructures as well as operational systems and middleware platforms (including application development tools, databases, and data analytics). On the other hand, customers (usually application developers) only control the installed applications and their configuration settings.

Finally, in the SaaS service model, CSPs provide customers with access to cloud applications hosted on the CSP's servers. Customers can use the CSP's applications (software) running on a cloud infrastructure without having to download or install them. In this model, customers do not control or manage the underlying cloud infrastructures, middleware platforms, or individual applications. All the underlying cloud infrastructures and deployed software related to the provision of the SaaS service are managed by CSPs. Well-known examples of the SaaS service include online communications services (e.g., Gmail and Messenger) and online productivity software (e.g., Microsoft Office 365).

Although CSPs typically categorise their services into these three types when they communicate with customers, it is important to recognise that the exact lines between each of these services are not easy to draw. While these categories are useful in understanding the whole concept of cloud services, they are more of a spectrum than hard and fast distinctions.[8] This means that, from the perspective of competition law, each service model does not necessarily constitute a relevant market by itself. There may be other effective substitutes, whether on-the-cloud or not, for each service, and they even have possibilities of substituting each other, which is an issue analysed in the CMA's recent working paper.[9] To better understand the cloud service market in the context of competition law and policy, this section attempts to identify several economic characteristics of cloud services, which plausibly explain the reason for the market's high concentrated structure.

Economies of Scale

Regardless of which kind of cloud services (IaaS, PaaS, SaaS, or a mixture of two or all of them) a CSP wants to offer, it needs servers, network equipment, and other infrastructure to enable its business activities. SaaS or PaaS CSPs may, to a certain degree, use other CSP's IaaS service, as an alternative to self-built infrastructure, to provide their services. On the other hand, a IaaS CSP generally need to build its own data centres and operate its own cloud computing infrastructure therein. It is thus undoubtedly that the infrastructure is essential in the provision of cloud services, from a CSP's standpoint.

The costs of building and maintaining data centres are high. They include costs of real estates, costs of the physical computing resources, operating costs, and energy costs. Economies of scale in the cloud services market is thus achieved in various ways. Regarding the supply-side economies of scale, CSPs benefit from economies of scale in energy costs, infrastructure labour costs, security and reliability, and increased buying power.[10] Also, they enjoy the demand-side economies of scale thanks to the virtualisation technology that allows sharing of computing, storage, and networking resources so that fewer servers are needed to carry the same workload.[11]

Apart from the economies of scale associated with computer resources, given the increasing need of cloud services, CSPs are making massive investments in research and development (R&D) to improve existing cloud services or to develop new cloud services. Given the virtualised and customisable nature of cloud services, the range of the cloud services provided by a CSP has a significant influence on its competitiveness. It is also observed that some CSPs invest substantial sums by means of acquisitions in order to expand their service range.[12] This implies that economies of scale can be achieved with investments in R&D. Developing an idea or a project in the cloud services sector can involve high R&D costs, but once it has been successfully developed, the marginal costs are relatively low compared to the R&D costs.[13] Further, new and better services attract more customers, and the more customers a CSP has, the more it can spread the R&D costs and provide the service at an attractive price because of the economies of scale.

Network Effects

In general, direct network effects emerge as more firms use the same cloud infrastructure provided by the same CSP. Indirect network effects arise when a large user base of the cloud infrastructure incentivises CSPs to optimise physical infrastructure and software for the cloud.[14]

As mentioned above, the cloud infrastructure constitutes an essential basis of all kinds of cloud services. It is thus natural for firms to prefer developing their B2B cloud services on the infrastructure of a dominant CSP which has the most business users. Specifically, such preference may result from a blend of reasons. Firstly, the potential sales market (marketplace) for their B2B services is greatest in the dominant CSP's cloud ecosystem. Secondly, if their services considerably rely on the transfer speed, e.g., time-critical services targeting the financial industry and data transport services, they may be more inclined to choose a dominant CSP as their development platform to minimise the time needed for the transfer, because there is high possibility that the dominant CSP's service is also being used by their potential customers. Thirdly, although cloud services from various CSPs are not necessarily interoperable, it would be theoretically easier to achieve interoperability among CSPs when they are all developing their cloud services on the same CSP platform. Therefore, when a potential customer is considering purchasing a cloud service, it has added value to the customer if the service provided by a third-party software vendor can be used in combination with services supplied by the CSPs from which they purchase most of their cloud services.[15,16]

Vertical Integration of Large CSPs

It is observed that Leading CSPs, namely Amazon, Microsoft, and Google, are providing integrated packages of different cloud services (IaaS, PaaS, and SaaS). For example, Amazon started its cloud services, i.e., Amazon Web Services (AWS), as an IaaS service, and gradually expanded its services to include PaaS and SaaS services. By contrast, Microsoft has long been in a strong market position in the

SaaS services it offers, such as online productivity software, and later extended its services to cover PaaS and IaaS services.

Usually, when a customer needs to integrate different kinds of cloud services, it has two options: (1) by having all the services interoperable, allowing these cloud services to connect and communicate; and (2) by running services provided by one single CSP.[17] However, interoperability may not be always guaranteed because not all CSPs disclose the APIs and standards of the services they provide. Even if the APIs and standards are provided, it takes efforts to deal with the connection issue and has risks of errors and compatibility issues. In such cases, purchasing integrated services from a single CSP seems to be a feasible and practical solution. Additionally, customers may obtain discounts if they purchase multiple cloud services from a single CSP. Such customer's need for one-stop shopping has been contributing to the vertical integration of CSPs.

Also, vertical integration enables CSPs to gather more information, including competitively significant data, through their customers in the marketplace.[18] They have first-hand information about usage metrics regarding any cloud service that runs on their own infrastructures, regardless of whether it was developed by themselves or third-party CSPs. From a third-party CSP's viewpoint, concerns thus arise because the CSP providing cloud infrastructures may take advantage of this information to make business decisions regarding which types of cloud services to acquire or replicate to offer by itself.

Barriers to Entry

With respect to the barriers to entry, the initial costs of a CSP are quite different depending on what kind of service model it provides. Yet, in most cases, a customer prefers to purchase cloud services from a CSP who offers various services, primarily because it might have the need to purchase other cloud services and want to connect the various cloud services afterwards without tackling the interoperability issue, as explained above. For new entrants, it seems unrealistic to start from scratch and compete with incumbent CSPs on all layers (software, platform, and infrastructure) simultaneously in the cloud services market.

For SaaS services, the barriers to entry are basically relatively low, because SaaS services are heterogeneous and new entrants can differentiate its SaaS services from that of its competitors in the market. Given the nature of SaaS services, a CSP focusing on providing SaaS services can purchase other CSP's PaaS and IaaS services to obtain the cloud infrastructures required to develop its SaaS services. The initial capital investments are thus low because in most cases the usage of cloud infrastructures is charged on a pay-as-you-go basis.[19] However, it may still be difficult for a CSP to develop a SaaS service and enter the market where rival SaaS services are already being provided. A lock-in effect, brand awareness, and the first-mover advantage are the main obstacles to market entry in such case.[20] Furthermore, in the case that the rival SaaS services are provided by a vertically integrated CSP, market entry may be difficult due to the vertically integrated CSP's anticompetitive practices, such as tying and bundling discounts.

As to PaaS services, they often focus on a specific form of development, such as web deployment, mobile deployment, and machine learning.[21] Given their technical nature of connectivity between applications and the cloud infrastructures on which they run, they are less diverse than SaaS services, and have less room for differentiation and innovation when compared to SaaS services. Because PaaS services are generally used as part of a chain of different services, interoperability between different services is of the most importance for PaaS services. This is especially true in the case where closed APIs and standards are adopted, and where the PaaS CSP lacks information on how other CSPs' infrastructures operate. Also, due to the same reason, it is common for CSPs to provide integrated cloud services involving PaaS services, and such integrated CSPs have a competitive advantage in providing PaaS services compared to those who provide only PaaS services. Such competitive advantage results from not only high interoperability but also economies of scale. Although the entry costs of PaaS services are relatively low compared to that of IaaS services given that the cloud infrastructures can be 'purchased' from other IaaS CSPs, as in the case of SaaS services, non-integrated PaaS CSPs have no cost-competitive advantages when their rivals are integrated CSPs owning cloud infrastructures.

Lastly, regarding IaaS services, they are the most homogenous service among the three types. Competition among IaaS CSPs is theoretically mainly on price. Owing to the economies of scale, as explained above, the existence of large global CSPs makes market entry difficult.[22] Apart from the economies of scale, technological leadership and reputation; and the costs and security risks of switching also lead to high entry barriers.[23] However, it is still possible for new entrants to enter the relatively small niche market.[24]

High Switching Costs/Vendor Lock-In[25]

It is observed that cloud service customers seldom change their CSPs after they decided to move from on-premise to the cloud environment.[26] Sophisticated reasons behind this 'lock-in' could be categorised into two types: technical switching barriers and financial switching barriers.

With respect to technical switching barriers, they consist of four situations: interconnectedness, different product offering, data portability, and multi-cloud.[27] Firstly, interconnectedness refers to a situation that customers have to spend time on re-writing codes to create or maintain the interconnection of all cloud services they use, as well as to train employees in charge of the cloud services to understand how the communication between the original and new services should be set up and managed if they want to switch to a new CSP. The more cloud services that are interconnected, the more complex and time-consuming it is to switch, regardless of the layer or layers involved. Secondly, different product offering means that there are always technical differences, e.g., different technical security or privacy standards, in the CSPs' product offerings despite the functional similarity among them. This implies that there is not always a ready alternative for a cloud service being used by customers. Thirdly, the data portability issue exists in the cases that the original or new CSP used closed APIs and standards, along with incompatible data formats, which raise hurdles to the transfer of data. Lastly, multi-cloud indicates the situation in which customers use similar cloud services provided by different CSPs in parallel. Although multi-cloud offers the possibility for customers to switch between different CSPs, it does not always effectively mitigate the lock-in effect; on the contrary, if the interoperability between different CSPs' cloud services is insufficient, multi-cloud might result in a de facto lock-in in multiple clouds in the end.[28] In such a situation, a single CSP is predominantly used, and services of other CSPs are only used for specific services for which no interconnection is needed.

On the other hand, financial switching barriers mainly include two kinds: egress fees and discounts (credits included). Egress fees are charges from CSPs for customers' moving or transferring data from the CSPs' cloud, while ingress fees are charges from CSPs for receiving data sent by customers. Currently, major CSPs do not impose ingress fees to their customers, but charge egress fees based on the amount of data transferred from their cloud if it exceeds the CSPs' free tier.[29] When customers want to switch to a new CSP, first they need to transfer their data from the original CSP's server to the new CSP's server. Customers must pay for this transfer under the name of 'egress fees', which are charged separately from the fees that customers pay for using CSP's computer resources. Because of this current pricing structure, the barrier to purchase a CSP's cloud service and then store data in its cloud is low. It may be, however, costly to migrate data from the original CSP's cloud, depending on how much data customers store on it. Since the volume of data stored by customers usually increases over time, the total egress fees also go up more in the course of time.[30] This pricing structure, where moving data out of the cloud is expensive due to the egress fees, thus discourages customer switching.

Another financial switching barrier is the discounts offered by CSPs for the purpose of incentivising their customers to commit to long-term usage of the CSPs' cloud services. The business practice of offering discounts, whether usage-based, fee-based, or a mixture of both, is widespread in the cloud services market.[31]. Such discounts, in conjunction with other switching disincentives, e.g., egress fees, encourage customers to concentrate their business with one provider to receive discounts, and consequently raise barriers to entry and expansion for smaller CSPs. The existence of discounts thus has an impact on customers' switching behaviour. Also, the complexity of calculating the amounts of discounts is another inconvenience with regards to customer's decision on the switching because they may find it difficult to directly compare pricing plans between CSPs.

The above-mentioned economic characteristics of cloud services favour larger CSPs, and lead to the high concentrated structure of the cloud services market.[32] As observed in the cloud services market, these characteristics lead to *competition for the market*, where major CSPs offer integrated ecosystems and compete based on different technical standards. Although the cloud services market is still in its rapid expansion period, the structural factors and potential anti-competitive practices by major CSPs have drawn many competition authorities' attention. Section III then briefly introduces competition authorities' market studies on the cloud services, as well as existing legislation introduced to address competition issues in the cloud services market.

Market Studies Relating to Cloud Services in the Competition Law Context

The cloud services market has been apparently on the rise in recent years. For example, according to Synergy Research Group, the worldwide market share of top three leading IaaS CSPs (Amazon, Microsoft, and Google) accounted for 66% (32%, 23%, and 12%, respectively) of the worldwide cloud market in the second quarter of 2024.[33] Many competition authorities, including US, UK, Netherlands, France, and Japan, have conducted market studies on the cloud services recently, partly because of the current oligopolistic market structure of the cloud services market. Although these market studies have minor differences in their study focus and recommendations since the competition status of the cloud services market varies in each country, they commonly expressed the competition authorities' concerns about anti-competitive practices therein. Apart from these market studies, new regulations were adopted in the EU to tackle competition issues in digital markets, including the cloud service market. These regulations, however, are criticised for, among other things, listing cloud services as a kind of core platform service[34] and for the lack of clarity.[35] Below we firstly provide an overview of market studies conducted by competition authorities and regulators, and then discuss the EU regulations related to cloud services.

In the US, the majority staff of the House Judiciary Subcommittee on Antitrust, Commercial and Administrative Law released an investigation report focusing on competition in digital markets in 2020. In this prominent report, the cloud computing is also included as one of the targeted markets.[36] Yet, the focus was mainly put on the IaaS service, particularly with regards to the marketplace and the anticompetitive use of data. Following this report, USFTC sought public comment on CSPs' business practices that could impact competition and data security in 2023. After hosting a panel discussion,[37] USFTC pointed out several key themes and posed a few questions in its blog post in November 2023.[38] With regards to competition, USFTC highlighted three issues: software licensing practices, egress fees, and minimum spend contracts. It seems that more attention is put on potential anticompetitive conduct rather than the market structure of cloud services in the US antitrust law context.

In Europe,[39] Netherlands[40] and France[41] governments also carried out market studies in 2022 and 2023. Autoriteit Consument & Markt (ACM), the Dutch competition authority, analysed the whole cloud services sector including the IaaS, PaaS, and SaaS layers in its report, emphasising two aspects in particular: competition for customers' initial choice of CSPs, which is associated with the customer's motivation to adopt multi-cloud strategies, and the issue of vendor lock-in, which stems from various kinds of switching barriers. Autorité de la concurrence, the French competition authority, focused mainly on IaaS and PaaS services, and analysed three types of related areas where dominant CSPs could leverage their market power: data centre colocation services, on-premise software, and intermediation in consulting and integration of cloud solutions.

The Office of Communications (OFCOM), the UK regulator for the communications industries, published its cloud services market report in October, 2023.[42] OFCOM also focused on cloud infrastructure services (IaaS and PaaS), finding that competition for customers to switch or use multi-cloud is, to a certain extent, limited by CSPs' commercial and technological practices, including egress fees, technical restrictions on interoperability and data portability, and committed spend discounts. OFCOM has referred the UK public cloud infrastructure services market to the Competition and Markets Authority (CMA) to carry out a market investigation. CMA is in the middle of its investigation at the moment, and has issued its issues statements twice in order to outline initial theories on what might be affecting competition and potential remedies.[43]

Turning to Asia, in 2022, Japan Fair Trade Commission (JFTC), the Japanese competition authority, conducted a survey regarding trade practices in the cloud services market, aiming to identify the trade practices by dominant CSPs and the competition status in Japan's cloud service sector. In its report,[44] the JFTC clearly pointed out that, while a certain level of competition on prices and quality in the cloud services market was observed, the market is highly likely to change into a noncompetitive structure in the future.[45] As to the potential anticompetitive conduct, the JFTC's report analysed CSP's egress fees, integration of different functions, CSP's self-preferencing for software licenses, and preferential treatment of exclusive partners. Compared to other competition authorities' market reports, the JFTC's report is intriguing as it also examined, under the Antimonopoly Act, several alleged anticompetitive conduct that takes place in the CSP's 'marketplace'.[46] This indeed helps to draw a line between acceptable and unacceptable business practices, which is desirable in the Japanese competition law context.

In addition to the regulator and competition authorities' reports mentioned above, there are two other research reports that attracted much attention. One is entitled 'Cloud Infrastructure Services: An analysis of potentially anti-competitive practices',[47] prepared by Frédéric Jenny for CISPE in 2021. This report listed several CSP's potential anticompetitive practices that are likely to occur in the cloud services market, such as bundling, tying, raising rival costs, self-preferencing, and their effects on innovation, and offered a theoretical assessment. The other is Centre on Regulation in Europe (CERRE)'s report,[48] which, published in 2024, provided a timely economic and legal assessment of the recently adopted policies and regulations as well as their justifications from an economic perspective. The legal assessment part, focusing on the interpretation of the relevant provisions of the Data Act (DA) and the Digital Markets Act (DMA), is informative and worth a read because the DA and the DMA's global regulatory influence, known as 'the Brussels Effect',[49] is on-going and far-reaching.

In brief, how the highly-concentrated market structure has been formed in the cloud service sector is a key issue that needs to be considered when tackling CSPs' anticompetitive conduct. Most of the competition authorities have noticed this issue and correspondingly expressed their concerns in their market reports. The DA and the DMA, discussed in the next part, are an ambitious endeavour, undertaken by the EU, to address the market structure issue.

EU Legislation on Cloud Computing Services: Facilitating Competition

Compared to other jurisdictions, the EU has taken the lead in adopting sector-specific rules for cloud services. In addition to Articles 101 and 102 of the Treaty on the Functioning of the European Union (TFEU), the EU has introduced the Digital Markets Act and the Data Act in 2022 and 2023, respectively. From the perspective of competition law and policy,[50] the DA and the DMA catch the authors' eye because of their substantial influences on CSP's competition in the foreseeable future. As explained above, economic characteristics of cloud services, especially economies of scale and high switching costs, have led to the high degree of market concentration in the cloud services market. Tackling anticompetitive practices in the cloud services market without addressing the structural issue underpinning these practices appears to address the symptom rather than the cause. The DA and the DMA, on the other hand, directly or indirectly address competition-related issues, the former dealing with switching and interoperability issues and the latter with fairness and contestability issues for specific core platform services including cloud computing services. With these issues being addressed, it is expected that the market concentration will decline and that the competition in the cloud services market will become fiercer as customers are able to switch between CSPs with less obstacles.

In this part, in order to understand the trend of regulating the cloud services market with ex ante and sector-specific regulations, instead of analysing the potential application of traditional competition law in the cloud services market,[51] which has been extensively and thoroughly analysed in the above-mentioned market studies, this chapter focuses on the DA and the DMA, explains their respective purpose and impact on the cloud services, and points out potential issues likely to arise following the introduction of such regulations.

Data Act (DA)[52]

The DA is a key pillar of the European data strategy,[53] in which the EU Commission announced the creation of Common European Data Spaces, a single market for data. To establish this data market, the DA aims to facilitate customer switching between data processing services (DPS) and to develop interoperability standards for data to be accessed, transferred and used.[54] This regulation has entered into force on 11th January 2024, and will become applicable in September 2025. Prior to the DA, the EU had adopted a self-regulatory approach to encouraging the switching of DPSs and the porting of data but found the self-regulatory approach ineffective.[55] The DA was thus adopted to accelerate the progress towards the creation of Common European Data Spaces.

Generally, the DA is applicable to CSPs when their cloud services meet the definition of DPS. IaaS, PaaS, and SaaS cloud services, in most cases, fall into the scope of the definition of DPS.[56] Therefore, the DA can be considered a sector-specific regulation for cloud services.[57] In this regard, there are two main categories of obligations worthy of note under the DA with respect to facilitating competition in the cloud services market. One is the obligations to remove obstacles to effective switching (provided mainly in Chapter VI), and the other is the obligations to promote interoperability between DPS providers (provided in Chapter VI and VIII).

Chapter VI of the DA, as indicated in the title of Article 23, aims to remove pre-commercial, commercial, technical, contractual, and organisational obstacles[58] to effective switching between DPSs.[59] Specifically, Chapter VI emphasises consumer protection in terms of contractual terms of DPS (Article 25), information provision duties (Article 26), obligation of good-faith in cooperation (Article 27), contractual transparency (Article 28), gradual elimination of switching charges (Article 29),[60] functional equivalence for IaaS services (Article 30), and interoperability for PaaS and SaaS services (Article 30). It should be noted, however, that switching obligations imposed on DPS providers are not limited to the situation where customers switch to a different DPS covering 'the same service type'. Other situations, involving switching to the customer's on-premises ICT infrastructure and adopting multi-cloud strategies, are also included.[61] In addition, the definition of 'the same service type' under the DA is also ambiguous. The 'same service type' of DPS means a set of DPSs that share the same primary objective, data processing service model, and main functionalities.[62] However, these factors are not related to the DPS's operational characteristics.[63] Put differently, providers of the DPS covering 'the same service type' are NOT necessarily rivals in a competition law sense – they may have different and competing characteristics such as performance, security, resilience, and quality of service. Based on this understanding, switching obligations under the DA are applicable in the cases of not only substitutable DPSs but also complementary DPSs. How to assess the overall impact of these switching obligations on the market competition thus remains a critical question to be addressed in future studies.

Given that interoperability is essential to the advent of a single market for data, Chapter VIII of the DA, together with Article 30, prescribes interoperability obligations.[64] To be specific, Chapter VIII sets out essential requirements regarding interoperability of data of data sharing mechanisms and services, as well as of common European data spaces (Article 33), interoperability obligations in the case of multi-cloud (Article 34), open interoperability specifications and harmonised standards for the interoperability of DPS (Article 35), and essential requirements for smart contracts for data sharing (Article 36).

Among all the obligations, Article 29 and 30 are particularly important with respect to competition in the cloud services market. Brief explanations are given in the following paragraphs.

Switching Charges

Firstly, Article 29 reflects the EU's attitudes towards switching fees – providers of DPS should not impose any switching charges on the customer for the switching process. Yet, given the current widespread practice of switching charges, a three-year transition period has been introduced to allow time for DPS providers. During the transition period, DPS providers can only impose switching charges that do not exceed the costs directly linked to the switching process concerned (Article 29(3)). This newly-introduced Article 29 is estimated to effectively lower the high switching costs, especially in terms of egress fees, to a significant extent. Without switching charges, it becomes easier and more predictable for customers to compare their current pricing plans with other DSP providers' plans, which effectively facilitates switching. There is however an exception to the obligations under Article 29. In the case of multi-cloud, the practice of charging egress fees may be allowed but only to the extent of egress costs incurred for the purposes of multi-cloud (Article 34(2)).[65]

Functional Equivalence and Interoperability

Secondly, Article 30 emphasises functional equivalence for IaaS services (para 1) and interoperability for PaaS and SaaS services (paras 2–4). Regarding functional equivalence for IaaS services, Article 30(1) provides that DPS providers must take all reasonable measures, after their customers switched to other DPSs covering the same service type, to facilitate the functional equivalence.[66] Under Article 30(1), IaaS CSPs is required to offer assistance and support to the customer within their capacity through providing capabilities, adequate information, documentation, technical support, and the necessary tools, rather than to develop new categories of DPSs or to rebuild their services within the destination DPS provider's infrastructure.[67] Concerning interoperability for PaaS and SaaS services, Article 30(2) provides that PaaS and SaaS service providers should "make open interfaces available to an equal extent to all their customers and the concerned destination providers of data processing services free of charge to facilitate the switching process", and Article 30(3) requires these providers to ensure compatibility with specifications based on open interoperability specifications or harmonised standards for interoperability.[68] Further, if open interoperability specifications or harmonised standards have not been identified yet, they are still obliged, when requested by the customer, to export all exportable data in a structured, commonly used and machine-readable format, under Article 30(4). By facilitating interoperability, the DA aims to "overcome vendor lock-in, which undermines competition and the development of new services".[69] These obligations (Article 30(2), 30 (3) and 30(4)) are also applicable, *mutatis mutandis*, to DPS providers in the case of multi-cloud (Article 34).

Some commentators suggest that the DA seems to purposely distinguish between horizontal interoperability (interoperability in the case of exchanging data between DPSs covering the same service type) and vertical interoperability (interoperability in the case of exchanging data between DPSs that are not of the same service type),[70] the former being guaranteed under Article 30 and the latter under Article 34.[71] However, since the exact wording in Article 34 is "in-parallel use of data processing services" rather than "in-parallel use of multiple data processing services with complementary functionalities", the expression of which is used in

Recital (99) of the DA, such interpretation, premised on the understanding that Article 34 only focuses on vertical interoperability in the context of multi-cloud, seems to be inconsistent with the wording of Article 34. How to precisely understand the relationship between Article 30 and 34 of the DA thus needs to be further clarified.

In sum, as concisely illustrated above, although the newly-introduced DA is leading to considerable changes in how cloud services are offered to customers, it still has various interpretation issues needed to be resolved.

Digital Markets Act (DMA)[72]

The DMA aims to ensure contestability and fairness for the markets in the digital sector. It empowers the EU Commission to designate undertakings as gatekeepers if their core platform services (CPS) constitute an important gateway between business users and consumers. Cloud computing services,[73] as a kind of CPS provided in Article 2(2)(i) of the DMA, therefore also fall under the scope of the DMA.

EU legislators have observed that EU competition law is not sufficient to tackle competition problems in digital markets because (a) the scope of Articles 101 and 102 of TFEU is limited to certain instances of market power, (b) enforcement of EU competition law occurs ex post and requires an extensive and time-consuming investigation on a case-by-case basis, and (c) gatekeepers are not necessarily dominant in the competition law meaning, and their conduct may not be effectively regulated under EU competition law.[74] The DMA thus serves as a complement to EU competition law.

Compared to the DA, which symmetrically applies to all CSP providers irrespective of size and market power, the DMA is an asymmetric regulation, imposing obligation only on the designated undertakings quantitatively and qualitatively qualifying as gatekeepers with respect to a specific CPS.[75] Once a CSP is designated as a gatekeeper by the EU Commission, it is subject to ex ante obligations under Articles 5 and 6 of the DMA. Article 5 contains a 'black list' of nine obligations, most of which are self-executing prohibitions, while Article 6 contains a 'grey list' of twelve obligations, measures of which may need to be further specified by the EU Commission pursuant to Article 8(2) of the DMA.[76] Although both lists generally apply to all designated gatekeepers irrespective of their business models and market characteristics, some of these obligations are tailored to specific CPSs or, and seem to be not applicable in the context of cloud computing.[77] The obligations under the DMA that are relevant to cloud computing services thus seem to be limited.[78]

Criticism for Regulating Cloud Computing Services under the DMA

In fact, some critics have pointed out that, unlike most of the other CPSs, cloud computing services are generally one-sided rather than multi-sided in nature.[79] Cloud computing services do not intermediate between business users and consumers; they provide SaaS, PaaS, IaaS, or a combination of these services to customers without functioning as an intermediary. According to the definition of a gatekeeper under Article 3(1)(b) of the DMA, a CPS must be "an important gateway for business users to reach end users". Cloud computing services, however, do not include such characteristics in most cases. Accordingly, whether the EU Commission would designate any influential CSP as a gatekeeper is an intriguing question which remains to be explored.[80] Even if the EU Commission designates any CSP with respect to cloud computing services and such designation is supported by the court, how to apply the above-mentioned obligations under Articles 5 and 6 of the DMA is another controversial issue.

In the case of marketplaces provided by CSPs, they indeed connect independent software vendors and end users via the marketplace, and exhibit indirect network effects. However, in view of their business characteristics, such marketplaces seem to satisfy the definition of 'software application stores' referred to in Article 2(14) and are more likely to be considered an online intermediation service (Article 2(2)(a)), instead of a cloud computing service (Article 2(2)(i)).

Potential Issues Concerning the Interplay of the DA and the DMA with Respect to Cloud Services

As described above, the DA could be considered a sector-specific regulation for cloud services, while the DMA provides for an ex ante regulation to complement competition rules, which mainly focuses on ex post enforcement in individual cases. To date, notwithstanding there are no gatekeepers designated for their cloud computing services under the DMA, the co-existence of these laws has brought about issues concerning their implementation.[81] These issues could be roughly divided into two aspects: substantive concerns and institutional concerns.

Regarding the substantive issues, how to interpret the relationship between the DMA and the DA is uncertain, as there are no explicit safeguards provided in the DA, which was adopted later than the DMA. By contrast, for example, Article 1(5) of the DA safeguards the application of Regulation (EU) 2016/679 (GDPR). It is thus unclear that, in the case of the overlap of application scopes between the DMA and the DA, which regulation should be prioritised, or, in other words, how to interpret relevant provisions to ensure coherence and consistency of the two regulations. For example, with respect to data portability obligations in the cloud service context, how to interpret Articles 25 and 26 of the DA and Article 6(9) of the DMA in a harmonised manner is a challenging issue, given that the DMA is an asymmetrical regulation and should in theory impose stricter obligations on gatekeepers compared to those symmetrically imposed on CSPs under the DA.

In this regard, the partial overlap of the core objectives of the two regulations needs to be taken into account in order to avoid normative overlaps and antinomies.[82] Article 5(3) of the DA, not necessarily in the cloud service context though, gives a good lead on how to coherently interpret relevant provisions. Article 5(3) of the DA prohibits gatekeepers under the DMA from requesting or obtaining access to user data generated by the use of a connected smart product or related service. The reason not to include gatekeepers as beneficiaries of the data access right is that, "(in) accordance with Regulation (EU) 2022/1925, and given the unrivalled ability of those undertakings to acquire data, it is not necessary to achieve the objective of this Regulation".[83] It thus could be said that the competition objectives defined in the DMA could be taken into consideration in the interpretation and enforcement of the DA. On the other hand, is it possible to implement the DMA with the objectives of DA in mind? In view of their regulatory features, namely the asymmetric DMA and the symmetrical DA, a plausible argument could be made that the DA provides the baseline for the interpretation and enforcement of the DMA. In any event, EU Cloud Rulebook,[84] a guideline providing extensive clarifications that may contribute to coherence and cross-consistency of all laws and regulations involved,[85] is desirable in order to minimise uncertainty.

Moreover, regarding the institutional concerns, the existence of multiple applicable regulations implies that multiple enforcement bodies govern the cloud service. The EU Commission is the sole enforcer of the DMA, while the high-level group may only provide advice and expertise on any general matter of implementation or enforcement of the DMA.[86] In contrast, the DA is enforced at a decentralised level, and potentially fragmented at national level if more than one competent authority is designated.[87] There is thus a risk that their parallel applications could lead to lack of coordination in the application of the respective regulation and result in various kinds of conflicts including legal inconsistencies. To address this potential risk, facilitating communications and cooperation among regulators is undoubtedly necessary, depending on to what degree the current coordination mechanisms articulated in the regulations function. Ultimately, an institutional redesign might be required to avoid the risk.

Conclusion and Outlook

In this chapter, we start with explaining the basic concepts of cloud computing and its service models, the IaaS, PaaS, and SaaS services, and then discuss the main economic characteristics of cloud services, including economies of scale (including two aspects: computer resources and R&D), network effects (mostly related to the marketplace provided by CSPs), the tendency of vertical integration (resulting from customer's needs for one-stop shopping and CSP's pursuit of competitiveness of its cloud ecosystem), high barriers to entry (especially in the PaaS and IaaS layers), and high switching costs (including technical and financial switching barriers), which cause the lock-in effects. These economic characteristics are the main determinants of the high concentration in the cloud services market, and many competition authorities have expressed their concerns about the oligopolistic structure of the cloud services market as well as anti-competitive practices therein. Through briefing reviewing these market studies, we confirm that the highly-concentrated market structure in the cloud services market is observed in most advanced jurisdictions, and that most competition authorities examine potential anti competitive practices, for example egress fees, that could be implemented by dominant CSPs to hinder competition to the detriment of cloud service users. In this regard, the EU has shown its determination to tackle competition issues arising in the cloud services market using a hard law approach. The DA and the DMA, as new regulatory approaches adopted by the EU, have a profound impact, whether negative or positive, on the competition in the cloud service market. Nevertheless, the DA has many questions needed to be pondered and answered to advance the understanding of this world-leading data legislation, while the DMA is being criticised because its regulatory framework seems inappropriate for cloud computing services, which in most cases do not intermediate between business users and end users. Moreover, there are also issues concerning the general relationship between the DMA and the DA, since their objectives substantially overlap and these two pieces of legislation have both introduced certain measures aimed to promote competition. It should be borne in mind that these issues, which could be categorised into those deriving from the 'one-size-fits-all' regulatory approach (for example, interoperability issues) and those arising from the involvement of multiple regulators, are not unique to the EU, but could occur in other jurisdictions where multiple competition-related laws apply to cloud services.

Whether to regulate cloud services under an ex ante competition-based regulation (not limited to a DMA-like regulation though), in addition to ex post competition law enforcement, is a crucial regulatory issue worthy of particular attention. Regulating cloud services without carefully taking their economic and industrial characteristics into account will undermine the uptake of technological innovation in the cloud service sector, and eventually jeopardise consumer interests. Yet, in view of 'the Brussels Effect' of the DA and the DMA, it is widely envisaged that similar regulatory initiatives may be introduced in other jurisdictions. As a timely example, in June 2024, Japan has enacted the Act on Promotion of Competition for Specified Smartphone Software (the Smartphone Act),[88] a corresponding Japanese version of the DMA, to tackle emerging competition issues in the Japanese smartphone market. Although CSPs are not subject to this Smartphone Act, which only applies to providers of mobile operating systems, application stores, browsers, and search engines, issues similar to the ones mentioned above (issues arising from the involvement of multiple regulators) have been observed. For example, the Smartphone Act provides justifications, including cybersecurity, privacy, juvenile protection, and other reasons specified by Cabinet Order, for specified software providers to rely on.[89] Compared to the DMA, the Smartphone Act is more flexible about the scope of justifications. Nevertheless, given that the JFTC, which also administers the Smartphone Act, does not specialise in cybersecurity, privacy, or juvenile protection matters, Article 43 of the Smartphone Act provides that the JFTC may request opinions on these matters from the relevant administrative bodies. However, in the case of conflict between two different legal ideologies, is it reasonable to expect that the JFTC, as an independent body, could make a fair and balanced ruling that reconciles competition with other legal values, rather than a ruling that gives priority to competition over other values? In any event, such a dilemma, arising from the involvement of multiple regulators can only be resolved with communications and cooperation among regulators.[90]

Notes

1 Microsoft completed its acquisition of Activision Blizzard on October 13 2023. https://www.sec.gov/ix?doc=/Archives/edgar/data/0000789019/000119312523255762/d537928d8k.htm. However, in the US, the FTC's administrative complaint is still pending before an administrative law judge, even though the Ninth Circuit Court denied the FTC's motion for an injunction pending appeal in July 2023. USFTC, Order Returning Matter to Adjudication, In the Matter of Microsoft Corp. and Activision Blizzard, Inc., Docket No. 9412 (Sep. 26, 2023).

2 CMA, Anticipated Acquisition by Microsoft of Activision Blizzard, Inc., Final report (Apr. 26, 2023), paras 8.1-8.442; USFTC, Administrative Complaint, In the Matter of Microsoft Corp. and Activision Blizzard, Inc., Docket No. 9412 (Dec. 8, 2022), paras 96–119.

3 Peter Mell and Timothy Grance, The NIST Definition of Cloud Computing Recommendations of the National Institute of Standards and Technology, NIST Special Publication 800-145 (Sept. 2011), p. 2.

4 For a recent example, it was reported in September 2024 that Japan Fair Trade Commission conducted an on-site inspection of the Tokyo office of VMware, a CSP globally known for its cloud system and service management software, on suspicion of tying and abuse of superior bargaining position. See NHK, https://www3.nhk.or.jp/news/html/20240925/k10014591481000.html (in Japanese). These anti-competitive practices may be a result of the vendor lock-in effect (explained in the following paragraphs) in the deployment of cloud.

5 Gary Biglaiser, Jacques Crémer and Andrea Mantovani, *The Economics of the Cloud*, TSE Working Paper, n. 24-1520 (Mar. 2024), p. 12.

6 Jigsaw Research, Cloud Services Market Investigation Qualitative Customer Research, Final Report (May 2024), para 7.3.1. https://assets.publishing.service.gov.uk/media/664f02634f29e1d07fadcd56/Cloud_Services_Market_Investigation_Qualitative_Customer_Research_Final_Report_.pdf

7 For more detailed definitions and examples of each service, see, Jigsaw Research, Cloud Services Market Investigation Qualitative Customer Research, para 2.2.7.

8 Alex Gaynor, Transcript of the FTC Panel Event on Cloud Computing: Taking Stock and Looking Ahead (May 11, 2023), p. 3. https://www.ftc.gov/system/files/ftc_gov/pdf/cloud-computing-taking-stock-and-looking-ahead-may-11-2023.pdf

9 CMA, Cloud Services Market Investigation: Competitive Landscape Working Paper (23 May, 2024), para 9.11. For a detailed explanation of this view, see paras 4.18–4.29.

10 Rolf Harms and Michael Yamartino, *The Economics of the Cloud*, Microsoft White Paper (Nov. 2010), pp 3–4. https://news.microsoft.com/download/archived/presskits/cloud/docs/The-Economics-of-the-Cloud.pdf

11 Rolf Harms and Michael Yamartino, *The Economics of the Cloud*, pp. 4–8.

12 Autoriteit Consument & Markt (ACM), Market Study Cloud Services, ACM/INT/440323 (Sep. 5, 2022), p. 47. https://www.acm.nl/system/files/documents/public-market-study-cloud-services.pdf

13 Autoriteit Consument & Markt (ACM), Market Study Cloud Services.

14 Biglaiser et al., supra note 5, pp. 40–41.

15 ACM, supra note 12, pp. 47–48.

16 In a market report prepared by Japan Fair Trade Commission, indirect network effects are further divided into two kinds: effects on introduction support businesses and effects on third-party software vendors. See JFTC, *Report on Fact-Finding Survey on Trade Practices by Digital Platform Operators: Report on Trade Practices in Cloud Services Sector* (June 2022), pp. 42–44. https://www.jftc.go.jp/en/pressreleases/yearly-2022/June/221102EN.pdf

17 ACM, supra note 12, pp. 20–21.

18 Subcommittee on Antitrust, Commercial and Administrative Law of the Committee on the Judiciary of the House of Representatives, Investigation of Competition in Digital Markets: Majority Staff Report and Recommendations (July 2022), p. 100. https://www.govinfo.gov/content/pkg/CPRT-117HPRT47832/pdf/CPRT-117HPRT47832.pdf
19 This means a flexible pricing model where users only need to pay for the computer resources they use. CSPs often charge their services according to a pay-as-you-go model rather than the tariff model used in traditional IT industries, which requires a one-time upfront payment for licenses.
20 ACM, supra note 12, p. 52.
21 ACM, supra note 12, p. 53.
22 Kamila Benzina, 'Cloud Infrastructure-as-a-Service as an Essential Facility: Market Structure, Competition, and the Need for Industry and Regulatory Solutions', *Berkeley Technology Law Journal*, Vol. 34 (2019), pp. 130–131.
23 Kamila Benzina, 'Cloud Infrastructure-as-a-Service as an Essential Facility', pp. 131–133.
24 ACM, supra note 12, pp. 51–52. Especially, because the services are provided through the cloud, data security and service reliability are much valued by customers. New entrants however usually do not have time-proven performance record to convince potential customers that they can provide reliable services compliant with industry-specific regulations.
25 Vendor lock-in refers to the situation where customers have difficulties in switching to the same kind of cloud services provided by other CSPs due to use of technologies specific to a CSP or complicated systems that have already been built on cloud services.
26 The JFTC's market survey revealed that, following a hypothetical 5–10% price increase of all the cloud services, only 4% of the respondents would switch back to on-premise. See, JFTC, supra note 16, pp. 37–38. Further, with a hypothetical 5–10% price increase of the cloud services, 85.9% of the respondents would continue using the same services; only 14.1% would switch to other cloud services or on-premise. JFTC, supra note 16, pp. 49–50. It seems empirically obvious that a lock-in effect is existing in the Japanese cloud services market.
27 ACM, supra note 12, pp. 55–57.
28 By contrast, there are also cases in which customers faced minimal challenges when using multiple public clouds due to the availability of open APIs, which make integration easier. See, CMA, *Cloud Services Market Investigation: Technical Barriers Working Paper* (June 6, 2024), para 4.14.
29 A pricing structure where ingress fees is free but egress fees has not always existed in the cloud services market. In fact, ingress fees had been charged by CSPs. For a history of the development of this pricing structure, see, ACM, supra note 12, pp. 58–59.
30 Jigsaw Research, supra note 6, para 5.2.4. et seq.
31 For a concise but thorough introduction to major CSPs' discount strategies, see, CMA, *Cloud Services Market Investigation: Committed Spend Agreements Working Paper* (May 23, 2024), paras 1.23–1.34.
32 Daniel Schnurr, Switching and Interoperability Between Data Processing Services in the Proposed Data Act, CERRE (Dec. 2022), pp. 8–9.
33 Synergy Research Group, 'Cloud Is a Global Market – Apart from China' (Aug. 21, 2024). https://www.srgresearch.com/articles/cloud-is-a-global-market-apart-from-china
34 Konstantina Bania and Damien Geradin, 'The Regulation of Cloud Computing: Why The European Union Failed to Get It Right', *Information & Communications Technology Law*, Vol. 33 Iss. 1 (2024), pp. 104–106.
35 Konstantina Bania and Damien Geradin, 'The Regulation of Cloud Computing', pp. 110–111.
36 Supra note 18, pp. 91–100.
37 USFTC, Cloud Computing: Taking Stock and Looking Ahead (May 11, 2023). https://www.ftc.gov/news-events/events/2023/05/cloud-computing-taking-stock-looking-ahead
38 USFTC, Cloud Computing RFI: What We Heard and Learned (Nov. 16, 2023). https://www.ftc.gov/policy/advocacy-research/tech-at-ftc/2023/11/cloud-computing-rfi-what-we-heard-learned

39 At the EU level, the European Parliament called on the European Commission to consider opening market investigations in the cloud service sector under the Digital Markets Act, given the highly-concentrated market structure in the single market. See European Parliament, Competition Policy? Annual Report 2023 (2023/2077(INI)), (Jan. 16, 2024). https://oeil.secure.europarl.europa.eu/oeil/popups/printsummary.pdf?id=1772334&l=en&t=E

40 ACM, supra note 12.

41 Autorité de la concurrence, Opinion 23-A-08 of 29 June 2023 on competition in the cloud sector (June 2023). https://www.autoritedelaconcurrence.fr/sites/default/files/attachments/2023-09/23a08_EN.pdf

42 Ofcom, *Cloud Services Market Study: Final Report* (Oct. 5, 2023). https://www.ofcom.org.uk/siteassets/resources/documents/consultations/category-3-4-weeks/244808-cloud-services-market-study/associated-documents/cloud-services-market-study-final-report.pdf

43 CMA, Public Cloud Infrastructure Services Market Investigation: Issues Statement (Oct. 17, 2023). https://assets.publishing.service.gov.uk/media/652e958b6972600014ccf9f6/Issues_statement__updated.pdf; CMA, Public Cloud Infrastructure Services Market Investigation: Updated Issues Statement (June 6, 2024). https://assets.publishing.service.gov.uk/media/66618c622605fac482e67be5/Updated_issues_statement.pdf

44 JFTC, supra note 16.

45 JFTC, supra note 16, pp. 53–54.

46 JFTC, supra note 16, pp. 86–90.

47 Frédéric Jenny, *Cloud Infrastructure Services: An Analysis of Potentially Anti-Competitive Practices*, CISPE (Oct. 2021).

48 Antonio Manganelli and Daniel Schnurr, *Competition and Regulation of Cloud Computing Services: Economic Analysis and Review of EU Policies*, CERRE (Feb. 2024).

49 The 'Brussels effect' is a term coined by Professor Anu Bradford describing the EU's unilateral power to regulate global matters through its legal institutions and standards. See Anu Bradford, 'The Brussels Effect', *Northwestern University Law Review*, Vol. 107, No. 1 (2012).

50 Although the Digital Services Act (DSA) also applies to cloud computing services when they qualify as hosting services, the application of the DSA has a limited impact on the cloud services market from a competition law perspective.

51 For an overview of the application of EU competition law to cloud computing services, see Niamh Gleeson and Ian Walden, '14 Facilitating Competition in the Cloud', Christopher Millard ed., *Cloud Computing Law*, 2nd edn, Oxford University Press, 2021, pp. 484–492.

52 Regulation (EU) 2023/2854.

53 Communication from the Commission to the European Parliament, the Council, the European Economic and Social Committee and the Committee of the Regions – A European Strategy for Data, COM/2020/66 final.

54 DA, Article 1(1)(d), and (f).

55 DA, Recital (79).

56 The definition of DPS, according to Article 2(8) of the DA, means a digital service that is provided to a customer and that enables ubiquitous and on-demand network access to a shared pool of configurable, scalable, and elastic computing resources of a centralized, distributed or highly distributed nature that can be rapidly provisioned and released with minimal management effort or service provider interaction. This definition covers numerous services with a range of different purposes, functionalities, and technical set-ups. See DA, Recital (81).

57 Manganelli and Schnurr, supra note 48, p. 29.

58 The obstacles are illustrated but not clearly defined under the DA though. According to Article 23 of the DA, when DPS providers prevent their customers from terminating the DPS contract, concluding a new DPS contract of the same service type, porting customer data and digital assets, achieving functional equivalence when customers use a new DPS of the same service type, or unbundling IaaS services from other DPSs, their

conduct may constitute an obstacle to effective switching and violate the DA. How to interpret Article 23 of the DA along with the subsequent provisions is thus a crucial issue for determining the scope of application.

59 It should be noted that Chapter VI of the DA applies to any data (including personal and non-personal ones) processed by DPS providers. See DA, Article1(2)(e).

60 According to Article 2(36) of the DA, 'switching charges' is defined as "charges, other than standard service fees or early termination penalties, imposed by a provider of data processing services on a customer for the actions mandated by this Regulation for switching to the system of a different provider or to on-premises ICT infrastructure." Switching charges include data egress fees (Article 2(35)), which constitute a financial switching barrier, as discussed above, but do not cover standard service fees or early termination penalties. Therefore, in the case where the cloud services are offered for a fixed duration, the CSPs may still impose proportionate early termination penalties on their customers. See Manganelli and Schnurr, supra note 48, pp. 32–33.

61 DA, Article 23.

62 DA, Article 2(9).

63 DA, Recital (81).

64 Article 2(40) of the DA defines interoperability as "the ability of two or more data spaces or communication networks, systems, connected products, applications, data processing services or components to exchange and use data in order to perform their functions."

65 For the justification of this exception, see DA, Recital (99).

66 For the definition of functional equivalence, see DA, Article 2(37).

67 DA, Recital (92).

68 For the detailed requirements of open interoperability specifications and harmonized standards for the interoperability of DPS, see DA, Article 35.

69 DA, Recital (90).

70 DA, Recital (90), n 75, p. 30.

71 Manganelli and Schnurr, supra note 48, p. 37. This distinction also seems dubious because of the vagueness and uncertainty of the definition of "same service type" under Article 2(9) of the DA.

72 Regulation (EU) 2022/1925.

73 The definition of 'cloud computing service' in the DMA means a digital service that enables access to a scalable and elastic pool of shareable computing resources, as defined in Article 4(19) of Directive (EU) 2016/1148.

74 DMA, Recital (5).

75 DMA, Article 3.

76 The terms 'black list' and 'grey list' are commonly used in terms of discussions on the gatekeeper's obligations and prohibitions under the DMA. For example, Alexandre de Streel, The European Proposal for a Digital Markets Act: A First Assessment, CERRE (Jan. 2021) pp. 16–18.

77 For example, the obligation under Article 6(11) seems to be only applicable to gatekeepers of online search engines. Likewise, the obligation under Article 6(12) seems to be applicable to gatekeepers of online intermediation services (software application stores), online search engines or online social networking services. In addition, considering that the ad-based business model has been rarely adopted by CSPs, obligations under Article5(2)(a), 5(9), 5(10), and 6(8) seem insignificant in the context of cloud computing services.

78 For an analysis of possible application of the DMA obligations in the context of cloud computing services, see Manganelli and Schnurr, supra note 48, pp. 47–50.

79 Bania and Geradin, supra note 34, pp. 104–105; Manganelli and Schnurr, supra note 48, p. 44.

80 To date, the EU commission has designated seven gatekeepers with respect to eight kinds of CPSs under the DMA, but no gatekeepers have been designated regarding cloud computing services and virtual assistants. See EU Commission, https://digital-markets-act.ec.europa.eu/gatekeepers_en (last visited Sep. 2024)

81 For a preliminary analysis of the relationship between the DA and the DMA, see Manganelli and Schnurr, supra note 48, pp. 53–58.
82 Manganelli and Schnurr, supra note 48, pp. 53–54.
83 DA, Recital (40).
84 DA, Recital (39).
85 EU competition law, GDPR, and other data-related laws and regulations (for example, the Data Governance Act) should be simultaneously taken into consideration in the EU context.
86 DMA, Article 40(5), 40(6) and 40(7).
87 DA, Article 37.
88 Act No. 58 of 2024. The Smartphone Act will come into force on December 19, 2025.
89 Article 7 of the Smartphone Act.
90 In this regard, guidelines that outline the JFTC's policies and principles regarding the factors to be taken into consideration may be instructive as a tool for increasing government transparency.

5 Regulation and Competition: A Study on Competition Regulation among Digital Platforms in China

Xiaofei Lu

Introduction

With the advancement of digital technology, the digital economy is expanding rapidly and significantly changing the global economy and society. Giant tech companies are improving convenience for users and consumers, spurring innovation, and leading economic and social development. It is estimated that by 2023, the digital economy will account for 60% of global gross domestic product (GDP), an increase of 8% from 2019. With the development of AI technology, the digital economy is expected to accelerate further.[1] However, with the rapid growth of these companies, legal challenges have emerged, including market monopolies, impediments to competition, and data breaches. Specifically, problems are emerging in the areas of competition law, privacy protection, intellectual property, and cybersecurity. The traditional legal framework has not adequately addressed the platform industry, where the competitive environment is diverse and volatile. Thus, countries worldwide are strengthening antitrust laws and ensuring fairness in digital markets. For example, the EU started applying its Digital Markets Act (DMA) and Digital Services Act (DSA) in 2024, strengthening regulations on giant tech companies. In the US, antitrust lawsuits against GAFA by the Department of Justice (DOJ) and state authorities are also increasing.[2]

On par with this global trend, China has been tightening its regulation of the platform economy since the late 1990s around tech companies such as Baidu, Alibaba, and Tencent (BAT) creating a huge ecosystem.[3] However, with rapid growth came anti-monopoly problems including the forced ‘pick one from two’ practice,[4] abuse of dominant positions, startup takeovers, market dominance through cash subsidies, and price discrimination using big data.[5] In 2021, Alibaba was fined a huge amount for its ‘pick one from two’ conduct. The company was fined a huge sum, attracting global attention as China’s first violation of platform anti-monopoly laws.[6] This incident triggered a rapid tightening of platform regulation in China and a series of anti-monopoly violation cases. Thus, it is expected that platform regulation in China will continue in the future. The Anti-Monopoly Law is moving from a period of inclusion and prudence[7] through one of tighter regulation to normalised supervision and control, with no signs of deregulation. Anti-Monopoly Law is considered an effective tool to protect fair

DOI: 10.4324/9781003489542-5

competition and technological innovation in the market.[8] In China, as in other countries, the limitations of conventional laws and regulations are recognised, and new approaches to dynamic competition are being sought. However, regulation is a double-edged sword, and depending on its application, it can undermine large companies' competitiveness and innovation.

This chapter provides an overview of platform regulation in China, focusing on competition law. First, it identifies the status and trends of relevant laws and regulations, and describes the overall legal and regulatory framework. Furthermore, it analyses changes in competition law and regulation, and clarifies the issues of approaches based on China's social culture and industrial policy. Next, issues in practice are highlighted through cases, and the governance of giant platforms and impact of laws and regulations are examined. Finally, the challenges faced by Chinese platforms and future prospects for laws and regulations are discussed.

Regulatory System for Digital Platforms in China: Anti-Monopoly Law

Legislative Framework of Platform-Related Regulations

At a press conference in June 2024, according to the State Council of China,

> China has so far enacted more than 150 laws and regulations in the network field, building a legal system with the Constitution as its foundation, laws and regulations as its support, traditional legislation as its foundation, and network-specific legislation as its core.

The establishment of the 'Four Liangs and Eight Pillars' (four pillars and eight beams) of China's network law and governance was highlighted, and institutional guarantees for the construction of a network powerhouse have been put in place.

Within this complex legal system, a specialised regulatory system has already been established for the giant platforms that support the digital Chinese ecosystem. Specifically, regarding competition law, in addition to the Anti-Monopoly Law, the Platform Guidelines issued by the Anti-Monopoly Committee of the State Council and the Anti-Unfair Competition Law are also applied. Furthermore, for data legislation, the Cyber Security Law, Data Security Law, and Personal Data Protection Law have been enacted. In terms of consumer protection, the Consumer Rights and Interests Protection Law and E-Commerce Law have been introduced. To protect intellectual property, patent and copyright laws exist, but these are mainly addressed in the Civil Code and E-Commerce Law. However, although these laws and regulations have different purposes and regulatory objectives, there is some overlap in content. In addition, numerous administrative regulations and normative documents address issues related to platforming. Thus, the laws and regulations intersect from multiple angles and comprehensively regulate the activities of platform companies.

Anti-Monopoly Law

China's Anti-Monopoly Law provides a similar system to that of other countries regarding abuse of dominant market position, business combinations, and cartels. However, some regulations prohibiting administrative agencies from abusing their administrative power are unique to China to eliminate or restrict competition (Article 10 of the Anti-Monopoly Law). The June 2022 amendment to China's Anti-Monopoly Law focuses on market monopolisation and oligopolisation by platforms.

Specifically, it prohibits the abuse of a market dominant position, with specific acts enumerated in Article 22(1). The 2022 amendment prohibits platform operators from abusing their market dominant position by using data, algorithms, technology, or platform rules (Article 22, Paragraph 2). In addition, the existing factors for recognising a market dominant position, such as market share, competitive conditions, financial strength, technical conditions, degree of dependence on other operators, and barriers to entry, are maintained (Article 23). Regarding business combinations, there were no provisions regarding platforms before the amendment of the law, but 'killer M&As' (mergers and acquisitions) by major platforms of startups and technology companies were frequent. Even if these acquisitions do not meet the sales declaration threshold, they will likely have anti-competitive effects due to their high market share in the relevant market. Therefore, the revised law stipulates that even if the business combination does not meet the declaration threshold, the monopoly law enforcement agency of the State Council may require the business operator to make a declaration if there is concern about competition exclusion or restriction effects (Article 26, Paragraph 2).

Thus, the revision of the Anti-Monopoly Law provides a legal basis for administrative investigations and judicial decisions by addressing monopolisation by platforms, newly regulating previously unregulated areas, and clarifying unclear points. However, in specific investigations and judgments, the authorisation methods and factors to be considered are not always clear. To complement this, the State Administration for Market Regulation (SAMR) promulgated relevant implementing regulations based on the Anti-Monopoly Law, which interpreted the Anti-Monopoly Law articles and detailed the certification factors in detail, thereby specifying how to address platform monopoly issues. This includes prohibiting monopolistic agreements, acts of abuse of a dominant market position, business combination review, acts of abuse of administrative power to exclude or restrict competition, and the abuse of intellectual property rights to exclude or restrict competition that came into effect in April 2023, August 2023, and January 2024.

The regulations include the State Council's regulations on notification standards for business concentration, which came into effect in January 2024. Together with the Anti-Monopoly Law, these sector-specific regulations form the regulatory framework governing platforms in China. Some were established before the revision of the Anti-Monopoly Law and were subsequently reviewed after its amendment. They play an important role in clarifying the enforcement standards and procedures of the Anti-Monopoly Law, preventing abusive market conduct, and maintaining market competition order.[9]

Notable among platform-related regulations is the 'Guidelines for Anti-Monopoly in the Platform Economy Sector' (Guidelines) promulgated by SAMR in February 2021. The Guidelines, consisting of 24 articles in 6 chapters, define platforms, providers, internal operators, etc.; delineate relevant markets; recognise the market dominant position (prohibition of 'pick one from two') and hub-and-spoke monopoly agreements; and provide provisions for the acquisition of start-ups. Considering the characteristics of the platform economy, the Guidelines focus on specific law enforcement and judicial decisions to promote fair competition, efficient supervision, stimulate innovation, and protect stakeholders' interests. In particular, for business combinations, the position of variable interest entities (VIE) schemes, which Chinese platform companies use to raise funds abroad while avoiding foreign investment restrictions, was unclear under Chinese law. However, Article 18 of the Guidelines clarifies for the first time that business combinations using such schemes are also subject to notification. This increased the number of disciplinary actions against related Gun Jumping.[10] Although the Guidelines are advisory and not legally binding, they set the direction for anti-monopoly regulation of platforms and marked the beginning of increased regulatory enforcement.

China's Anti-Monopoly Law was amended to adapt to the digital economy, and alongside the provisions and guidelines issued by the SAMR, a platform-specific anti-monopoly regulatory system has been established. While difficult to frequently amend the Anti-Monopoly Law to maintain legal stability and predictability, timely review of the provisions by the SAMR is necessary to respond to global changes and national industrial policies and to ensure flexibility in the application of the global enforcement of the law. However, the concentration of competition authorities' authority may increase the risk of abuse thereof and arbitrary interpretation of the law. Thus, the challenge is how to ensure fairness, transparency, and stability in enforcing the law in the platform area.[11]

Anti-Unfair Competition Law

In China, the Anti-Unfair Competition Law also plays an important role in regulating competition against platforms. Promulgated in 1993, this Law, which was amended in 2017 and 2019. Article 2 (2019), obligates operators to comply with the law and commercial ethics according to the principles of free will, equality, fairness, and good faith and credit in their production and management activities. It also prohibits acts that damage the legitimate rights and interests of other operators and consumers, as well as the use of technology in the network field, as stipulated in Article 12, to fraudulently interfere with the management of other operators. As such, Articles 2 and 12 regulate acts of unfair competition by platform operators, even if they do not fall under the acts enumerated in the respective articles.[12] In practice, the Anti-Unfair Competition Law addressed competition issues on platforms before the Anti-Monopoly Law.

For example, in a 2017 case in which the online food sales platform Meituan used its superior position to prohibit stall operators from opening shops on food delivery platforms Elema and Baiduwaimai, the Zhejiang Jinhua Municipal Supervision and Administration Bureau violated the restriction of competition regulations by punishing Meituan.[13] Such 'pick one from two' conduct has been subject to administrative punishment under Article 12 since the 2019 amendment of the Law.[14] Because the Anti-Unfair Competition Law does not require finding a 'dominant position in the relevant market', it is less of a hurdle to apply than the Anti-Monopoly Law; thus, the Anti-Unfair Competition Law is often applied at the local level when difficult to prove a dominant market position.[15] However, the level of fines under this Law is low, and its substantive deterrent effect against giant platforms is weak.[16] In addition, the Anti-Unfair Competition Law plays a significant role in both the areas of competition and in the protection of trade secrets and intellectual property rights. For example, this Law addresses the protection of big data and technical information, and disputes regarding trademark and patent infringement in e-commerce.[17]

However, the broad regulatory scope of the Anti-Unfair Competition Law and the unclear boundaries with other laws have been problematic.[18] In 2022, a draft amendment to the Law was released to regulate unfair practices related to online services on platforms. The proposed amendment prohibits the abuse of data, algorithms, and technological advantages to restrict competition, and requires that operators are responsible for complying with the law. Nevertheless, the proposed amendment has been subjected to criticism from both the practice and academic communities and has yet to be passed. Instead, SAMR promulgated the Interim Regulation on the Prevention of Network Unfair Competition in May 2024, which will take effect in September of the same year. This regulation organised conducts of unfair competition through the network and strengthened platforms' responsibility to manage their own platforms and regarding the abuse of data and algorithms. It also clarified the policy for handling violations based on the Anti-Monopoly Law and the Anti-Unfair Competition Law.

E-Commerce Law

China is the world's largest e-commerce market, and online transactions are expanding rapidly, led by major platforms such as Alibaba and JD.com. However, problems such as the protection of consumer rights, infringement of intellectual property rights, fraud, and acts restricting competition have emerged. Specifically, fraudulent activities such as fictitious transactions and fabricated user evaluations (including the lowering of competitors' ratings) are rampant, and the emergence of numerous companies that undertake these activities has become a serious social problem. In addition, prior to the 2022 amendment to the Anti-Monopoly Law, exclusive transactions involving platform-based competition were insufficiently regulated. Thus, demand grew for the enactment of regulations for this area. Against this backdrop, the E-Commerce Law was enacted in 2019 to regulate the e-commerce market, protect consumers, and promote fair competition.

Consequently, platforms are now required to examine and register merchants' qualifications, protect consumers, secure transactions, disclose information, prevent false advertising, clarify rules for impounding money, prevent the abuse of market dominance, protect intellectual property rights, and be responsible for providing secure electronic payment services. The E-Commerce Law complements the Anti-Monopoly and Unfair Competition Prevent Laws (Articles 22, 35, and 82),[19] as all three regulate "pick one from two" conduct. Some argue prioritising the E-Commerce Law over the Anti-Monopoly Law. However, the 'pick one from two' regulation in Article 35 does not make the existence of a dominant market position a requirement and judges the illegality of the conduct in question based on whether it is 'reasonable'. However, the criteria are vague. Furthermore, as with the Anti-Unfair Competition Law, fines and damages for illegal acts are low, acting as a weak deterrent for giant platforms; thus, few examples exist of its application in practice.[20]

The Anti-Monopoly Law, Anti-Unfair Competition Law, and E-Commerce Law all regulate the competitive conduct of platforms, leading to potential legal conflicts. The question of which law should apply to 'pick one from two' practices is actively debated in China. While some argue that the applicable law should be determined based on the plaintiff's complaint,[21] the court is required to conduct an appropriate legal analysis based on factual findings to ensure the application of the law is not arbitrary. For example, when the Galanz Group sued Alibaba's Tmall for anti-monopoly violations in 2019, it was argued that the sharp decrease in traffic on Tmall and its removal from in-app searches after partnering with Pinduoduo was due to the 'pick one from two' practice. Galanz eventually settled with Tmall and dropped the lawsuit, but it was noted that in this case, the Anti-Monopoly Law, rather than the E-Commerce Law, was applicable and was used as leverage in negotiations with Tmall.[22]

Although the criteria for the application of these three laws remain ambiguous and are not detailed in this chapter, the requirements of the 'pick one from two' conduct must be analysed considering the legal interests each law protects, as shown in Table 5.1. It would be appropriate to apply the Anti-Monopoly Law preferentially if the requirements for its application are met, and to consider the application of the other two if they are not. In addition, although the application of the Anti-Monopoly Law is prioritised in China, a departure from the current situation where the Anti-Unfair Competition Law is frequently applied, and the E-Commerce Law is not being sought.

Three Data Laws

China's 'Three Data Laws' – the Cyber Security Law (effective 2017), Data Security Law (effective 2021), and Personal Data Protection Law (effective 2021) – significantly impact digital platforms.[23] These laws introduced strict regulations on data protection, management, and privacy based on China's unique state-driven governance model. All platforms are required to operate in accordance with these regulations and with the will of the state while strengthening data compliance.

Table 5.1 Comparison of Anti-Monopoly Law, Anti-Unfair Competition Law, and E-Commerce Law

Legal Name	*Main Objectives & Characteristics*	*Applicable Situations*	*Application Requirements*	*Liability Rules (Admin Penalties Comparison)*
Anti-Monopoly Law	Ensure fair competition; resilient	Severe monopolistic conduct disrupting competition	Requires market dominance finding	Cease illegal activities; fines 1%–10% of sales; civil damages
Anti-Unfair Competition Law	Legitimate competition; low application hurdles	Acts damaging competition, not under Anti-Monopoly Law	Violated commercial ethics, destroyed fairness	Cease activities; fines $14,000–$70,000, up to $410,000 for severe cases
E-Commerce Law	Fair transactions; emphasis on platformer responsibility	Platform's fraudulent behaviour damages businesses within the platform	Superior platform position, unreasonable behaviour	Cease activities; fines $5,000–$70,000, up to $280,000 for severe cases

Source: Author's own creation.

First, the Cybersecurity Law aims to protect Internet infrastructure and data in China. The law goes beyond mere cybersecurity measures, establishing a state control framework for the Internet and requiring strict security measures for digital platforms from a national security perspective. It includes a safety assessment system for domestic data localisation and restrictions on cross-border data transfers, requirements for data monitoring and access by authorities, and obligates companies to store data domestically and cooperate with authorities. The law demonstrates China's commitment to establishing 'cyber sovereignty' in cyberspace.

Second, the Data Security Law was enacted to establish state control over the distribution, collection, and use of the data itself, or 'data sovereignty'. This law requires platformers to classify data according to their impact on national security and economic development, and to establish a management system according to their importance. Specifically, strict security regimes are required for handling data that are critical to protecting national security, public interests, and personal interests. Furthermore, the state clarifies that data management and use is to be employed as a strategic industrial policy to develop the digital economy and increase the nation's competitiveness.[24]

Third, regarding the Personal Data Protection Law, privacy awareness has traditionally been low in China, but with the development of the digital society, the use of personal information has increased, as has the problem of privacy violation. In 2018, Baidu founder Robin Li said he would 'trade privacy for convenience', causing an uproar among users.[25] This increased privacy awareness and the enactment of the Privacy Act of 2021. This law imposes strict obligations on platformers regarding obtaining user consent, data minimisation, respect for user rights, data localisation, and cross-border data transfers. It also positions platformers that provide complex services with a large number of users as 'gatekeepers' – with reference to the EU's DMA and DSA – and requires them to have compliance systems in place and supervision from an independent body (Article 58). However, where state interests and security are prioritised, platforms can access and monitor the personal information they collect, limiting true privacy protection.[26]

These three data laws are more than just a theoretical framework; they are rigorously applied and have significantly impacted Chinese platformers. For example, Alibaba has revised its privacy policy and strengthened its data management system to ensure users' personal information is handled appropriately. Regular audits and regulations by the authorities rigorously assess whether these measures comply with legal and regulatory requirements.[27] Tencent has also strengthened its data encryption and established an information security management system to ensure the safety of user information.[28] However, these efforts have increased compliance costs and the risk of international reputation damage, requiring platformers to strike a difficult balance.

Unlike the EU and US, China's data regulatory approach is state-centric and 'a unique combination of data protection and authorities' control over data flow'.[29] In an environment emphasising national security, cyber sovereignty, and data sovereignty, platformers face the dilemma of whether to 'root deep or deploy wide'. For example, the issues surrounding TikTok have revealed domestic and international regulatory risks, as parent company ByteDance was forced to sell its business in the US. In addition, the US, Canada, EU, and UK have further banned TikTok on official devices.[30] Thus, Chinese platformers are being forced to establish a difficult balance between legal compliance and maintaining user trust to adapt to the unique regulatory environment.

Considerations

In both the Anti-Monopoly Law and the Three Data Laws, China places significant emphasis on data sensitivity, and the regulation of platforms is heavily influenced by industrial policy, with a strong focus on state intervention and control. While the involvement of state power is necessary, as noted in the discussion on legal and regulatory transition below, if the scope of state power exceeds reasonable limits, legal stability and transparency will be undermined, business freedom restricted, and innovation curtailed, raising concerns that market competition will be reduced. For example, unrestricted state access to corporate data and monitoring of personal information for national security reasons could infringe on individual privacy and freedom. Thus, there is an undeniable risk of excessive monitoring of individual behaviour and restrictions on freedom of expression and freedom of thought.

Furthermore, the lack of corporate independence is a concern. Companies would be required to follow state directives in data management and operating policies, making independent decision-making difficult. In addition, from an international perspective, Chinese platformers are caught between different domestic and international regulations, and the strictness and rigidity of China's data regulations compared to those of other countries may require complex compliance responses, which could undermine international competitiveness.[31] For example, in February 2023, dozens of environmental, social, and governance (ESG) funds sold over US$1 billion worth of Tencent shares in a six-month period driven by concerns about censorship and regulatory risk from China.[32]

However, despite strict and fluctuating regulations, Chinese platformers have not taken a stand against the authorities, obeying the regulations and actively cooperating with authorities' requests. This can be attributed to several factors. The first is the size of the market and its economic benefits. The Chinese market has one of the largest Internet user bases worldwide, and it is very profitable for platformers to operate in mainland China. Therefore, to protect these interests, companies are trying to avoid confrontation with the authorities and comply with regulations to take advantage of opportunities to continue and expand their business.

Another major factor is the power relationship between the state and corporations in China. In China, there is a characteristic structure in which the state has overwhelming power and companies operate under its influence. In particular, strong regulations are in place for corporate operations and data management through data-related regulations. This legal framework not only puts companies at risk of serious sanctions and penalties if they violate the regulations, but also makes it impossible for them to easily rebel, as the authorities' surveillance extends to every corner of the country through data localisation regulations and other measures.

Third, platformers and authorities use each other in various areas and cooperate closely. Platforms work alongside the state in the economic, political, and social sectors to strengthen their influence. Economically, these companies play an important role in building market institutions (enforcing contracts and preventing fraud), enforcing laws (Alibaba and JD.com help the Supreme Court enforce debt repayment), experimenting with policies (Alibaba and Tencent partnered with local governments to help build 'smart cities'), and promoting rural development (Alibaba and Tencent). More recently, Alipay and WeChat Pay have been actively involved in new policy goals such as the addition of a Central Bank Digital Currency (CBDC)[33] and promotion of digitalisation in rural areas, further increasing their economic impact.

Politically, social media platforms and technology companies are helping to strengthen state surveillance and censorship activities, and helping to implement smart governance. Socially, during the Covid-19 pandemic, Alibaba and Tencent worked with local governments to develop and implement the contact tracking app 'Health Code' to ensure that infected individuals were tracked and quarantined, helping to contain the pandemic. In this way, extensive cooperation between the state and Big Tech companies is addressing governance challenges that the state alone cannot address. This process is termed 'institutional outsourcing'.[34,]

Chinese authorities rely on the power of giant platforms to transform the economic structure, construct a science and technology powerhouse, and leverage digital technology to drive national governance. Through this national strategy, the authorities are actively encouraging platformers to participate in key projects and industrial policies. Furthermore, platformers must maintain cooperative relationships to secure access to large markets and support from the authorities, and they need to be flexible and adaptable to increasing government pressures and regulations. Thus, platformers have established and grown their market position by maintaining cooperative relationships with governments, but at the cost of being forced to comply with government policies and regulations. This interdependence keeps platformers docile, but also contributes to the authorities' policy changes. Platforms are constantly seeking to adapt to China's unique regulatory environment while developing in constant tension between the pursuit of profit in the marketplace, international trust, and the authorities' regulations.

Historical Evolution of Competition Regulation over Platforms and Causes[35]

2008–2020: Inclusive and Cautious Phase

Overview

China's first comprehensive competition law, the Anti-Monopoly Law, was passed in 2008 during the transition from a Soviet-style planned economy to a market economy. Amid China's rapid economic development, the Anti-Monopoly Law emerged relatively late compared to other laws, and was introduced out of concern over the monopolisation of the Chinese market by multinational corporations. At the time, there was little competition in China's domestic capital markets to protect, and the Anti-Monopoly Law became a tool for powerful established companies to leverage state power to exclude competitors.[36] Subsequently, competition in the Chinese market intensified as state-owned enterprises reformed and industrial policies were promoted in the high-tech and innovation sectors. However, the factors that created a vigorous competitive environment were not so much the application of competition laws but the stimulation of various industrial policies by the authorities. China emphasised the role of the market and introduced private capital into state-owned enterprises while strengthening state control in key industries. Furthermore, anti-monopoly and competition policy in the Chinese market at the time was in a tug-of-war between forces promoting market competition and those protecting competitors favoured by the state.[37]

The emergence of platforms has fundamentally changed China's competitive environment, and since the 2010s, the country has recognised the importance of platforms and adopted various industrial policies to promote their development. For example, since 2015, it has actively promoted the 'Internet +' project, which aims to form a rudimentary 'Internet +' industrial ecosystem by 2025 that is cyber-oriented, intelligent, service-oriented, and cooperative. In this 'open and inclusive entry and management environment', private digital platform companies such as Alibaba have grown into giant tech companies through fierce competition.

This growth was supported by active promotion through industrial policy and by the inability of traditional regulation to cope with the rapidity, versatility, and complexity of digital platform growth, i.e., lax regulation. For many years, China was lax in applying and enforcing its antitrust laws against platforms, with enforcement agencies taking minimal formal action on complaints or reports of monopolistic conduct. Until 2020, competition law regulation for major platforms was virtually non-existent.[38] Although others such as the Anti-Unfair Competition Law dealt with the abuse of a dominant market position,[39] there was never a SAMR or court decision against a platform company under the Anti-Monopoly Law.[40] In addition, regarding business combinations, there were many business integrations of platform companies, but no review by competition authorities. Since there were no clear laws and regulations and judgment criteria, the courts failed to recognise plaintiffs' claims in monopoly dispute cases or took a long time to issue judgments.[41] This led to the free development of platforming in a lawless environment, undermining consumer interests and stifling fair competition and potential innovation.

Furthermore, although the Anti-Monopoly Law was not enforced, regulations are being developed in other areas of competition law: the Anti-Unfair Competition Law was amended in 2017, Cybersecurity Law was enacted in 2016, and E-Commerce Law in 2019. The same year, SAMR promulgated the Temporary Regulation Prohibiting the Abuse of a Dominant Market Position (repealed in 2023) as a guideline for the Anti-Monopoly Law. In addition, the Guiding Opinions on Promoting the Regular and Healthy Development of Platforms promulgated by the State Council Office in 2019, introduced innovative supervision principles and methods and highlighted conducting inclusive and prudent supervision of the platform domain. This policy included an 'observation period' in the short term and no immediate strict crackdown, indicating its inclusive and prudent attitude.[42]

Considerations

In addition to the characteristics shared by tech companies in other countries, such as two-sided and multi-sided markets, and the generation and use of data, factors unique to China have contributed to their rapid and large-scale growth in the country. First, China has a huge population and market unmatched by other countries. There is also strong competition policy support from the Chinese authorities, and since US tech companies like Google and Meta have been shut out of the Chinese market, there is little threat from foreign capital. In addition, the support of IT policies, with 'Internet+' at its core, is facilitating the growth of tech companies. Furthermore, many Chinese tech companies such as Alibaba are private and have innovated through ingenuity.

In corporate law in China, to facilitate high innovation in emerging industries, a 'first-launch, second-pass' approach is adopted in which companies and industries are left to their own devices and even legally grey areas are tacitly approved. This has enabled tech companies to grow significantly in an inclusive environment in which they try first and then are regulated as needed. On the other hand, through the ecosystem, these tech companies have actively solved the 'problems of Chinese society', such as improving the convenience of living by enhancing underdeveloped retail and public transportation, creating employment and learning opportunities, eliminating regional disparities, and improving social credit problems.[43] They have also served as good partners to the authorities. In this way, digital platforms have grown in China, taking advantage of economies of scale and the role of the authorities.

This inclusiveness and prudence has provided digital platforms the space for innovation and trial and error, while carefully and appropriately regulating the legal issues emerging with their development without over-regulation. Here, 'careful regulation' is based on law. As mentioned, the Chinese competition authorities rarely enforced the law against platforms for anti-monopoly violations until 2020; thus, it is questionable whether this inclusiveness and prudence remains meaningful today.[44]

2020–2022: Period of Tighter Regulation

Overview

While China reportedly tightened regulations on platforms at once from the end of 2020, in reality, the signs emerged in 2019. In November 2019, SAMR convened an Internet Management Guidance Roundtable, where they stated the illegality of 'pick one from two' and other illegal practices. In the fintech industry, Jack Ma publicly criticised state-owned banks and the financial system as he prepared to separate Ant Financial from Alibaba in October 2020. In response, in November 2020, the Central Bank, the Banking and Insurance Supervisory and Administration Commission, and other financial regulators interviewed the effective controlling person of Alibaba-affiliated Ant Financial Group and subsequently delayed Ant's listing application. This was supposedly to prevent threats to the competitiveness of the traditional banking industry and spread of Alibaba's monopolistic practices, unfair trading, unauthorised conduct of business, and other abuses in financial markets.[45]

Subsequently, in December 2020, the Central Political Bureau meeting established a policy to tighten regulations on platform operators to strengthen anti-monopoly efforts and prevent the expansion of capital anarchy. With this, the tightening of regulations began in earnest. In 2021, the SAMR's Guidelines and the Central Reform and Comprehensive Deepening Commission's 'Opinions on Strengthening Anti-Monopoly and Fair Competition Policy Implementation' were issued. Furthermore, in 2021, SAMR issued the 'Guidelines for Platform Classification', which ranks platform companies into super, large, and small and medium platforms according to size. In addition, a draft of the 'Internet Guidelines for Ensuring Platforms' Entity Responsibility' was promulgated and comments were requested. These guidelines were enacted with reference to the EU's DMA and DSA, but no further progress has yet been made. While they serve to encourage voluntary compliance by companies, their effectiveness and significance remain unclear.[46]

The law enforcement regime has also changed significantly. When the Anti-Monopoly Law was first passed, three agencies were responsible for its enforcement: the National Development and Reform Commission, Ministry of Commerce, and former State Administration for Industry and Commerce.[47] The Anti-Monopoly Law was not a government priority, and the dispersion of enforcement agencies and insufficient staff capacity were problems. However, the 2018 reform of the state structure established the SAMR and centralised antitrust enforcement authority. While this consolidation is expected to facilitate the smooth functioning of the competition law regime and more effective implementation of government orders, it has been emphasised that it may protect competitors favoured by the state when the goal is to implement broad socioeconomic rather than competition policies. In November 2021, SAMR's internal organisation reorganised to include the State Anti-Monopoly Bureau (SAMB), which includes three divisions in charge of cartel, abuse of dominant market position, and business combination cases, each reporting directly to SAMR. This reform is expected to improve the independence and effectiveness of competition regulation, but reportedly, its goal is to promote competition policy.[48]

Under the new regime, the SAMR investigated and strictly enforced anti-monopoly violations against numerous platform companies – 175 cases of various anti-monopoly violations in 2021, marking a 61.5% year-on-year increase. Of these cases, 92 were platform-related, with fines imposed. The fines and illegal amounts collected totalled approximately RMB 23.6 billion (China Anti-Monopoly Enforcement Annual Report, 2021). For example, regarding the abuse of dominant position, following the Alibaba case, Meituan was investigated in April and found to have abused its dominant market position in October, resulting in a fine of RMB 3.4 billion. The company was found to have used its dominant position in the market for online food delivery platforms in China in a 'pick one from two' practice by forcing trading operators to sign exclusive partnership agreements and by monitoring store openings on competing platforms.[49]

Dozens of platform companies were also fined for failing to give advance notice of business combinations. In July 2021, SAMR banned the merger of Tencent-owned online gaming platform Huya and live-streaming platform Douyu. This was because no problem-solving measures were proposed, as the merger, if implemented, would further strengthen Tencent's dominant market position and eliminate competition.[50] This is the first business combination prohibition case against a Chinese platform company and as important as the Alibaba one. That same month, Tencent was ordered to take measures to restore competition order, including abandoning its monopoly on music copyrights, and was fined RMB 500,000 for violating its notification obligations.[51]

Considerations

During this period, the authorities launched full-scale antitrust-related investigations against platform companies, tightened restrictions on the provision of financial services by platforms, and strengthened oversight of data management.[52] This strict regulatory content and proactive regulatory activities curbed the harmful effects of platform firms' excessive growth and their compliance awareness seems to have grown. Several factors can be cited as reasons for this regulatory effect.

First, the development and revision of regulations covering platforms has significantly improved their effectiveness and the regulatory capacity of competition authorities has improved. As a result of the strengthening of regulatory agencies and addition of specialised personnel familiar with the characteristics of the platform industry and antitrust regulation, administrative penalty decisions now include logical explanations aligned with guidelines, and transparency and fairness in the application of antitrust laws have been significantly enhanced.

The most important factor is a change in state competition policy to 'deter the uncontrolled expansion of capital' and a willingness to tighten regulations. In China, regulations are commonly tightened *en masse* when problems become more serious to create a show-off effect. Thus, it is likely that the tightening of regulations at this time was foreseen as a result of the fact that giant platform companies would be subject to the regulations. This tightening is common in Japan, the US, and Europe. Considering the 'winner-take-all' nature of the digital platform market, China's regulations are a natural progression. In fact, China's anti-monopoly authorities are taking a more cautious approach compared to the West, limiting penalties mainly to fines and avoiding corporate divestitures to minimise the negative impact on entrepreneurship and innovation.[53]

On the other hand, this tightening of regulations has significantly impacted the platform industry as a whole. According to a recent empirical study, the tightening of platform regulations in China did not promote competition as expected but suppressed it. The regulations have decreased venture capital investment in platforms and made startups hesitant to enter the market, reducing their numbers.[54]

Background and Factors Underlying the Change in Direction

- The change in direction aims to curb the harmful effects from a legal perspective. China's platform economy has reached a scale comparable to that of the US through rapid development and diversification of services, but the adverse effects of monopolies and oligopolies have had a significant negative impact on society. In response, China has tightened regulations in line with international actions. The change is also to eliminate threats to government's governance. China's private platformers have amassed power and resources far beyond the authorities' expectations and have significantly influenced political, social, and economic markets, and even public opinion.[55] This has led the Chinese authorities to recognise the potential of these platforms to threaten the political establishment, and thus, to tighten regulations.[56]
- It also aims to protect state-owned enterprises. While these are losing their competitive edge in the market, private digital platforms are growing rapidly and establishing dominant positions. This situation weakens the role of state-owned enterprises in the market, which the government is trying to maintain by curbing platform companies through new regulatory measures.[57] The change has also been linked to the pandemic.[58] Consequent to the significant deterioration of China's economic situation and the fact that national security, social stability, and sustainable economic growth have become all important, the government

has prioritised stabilisation over the further development of the digital economy, and has therefore tightened regulations.

Was the Tightening of Regulations 'Sudden'?

Based on the above, 'abrupt' may not be appropriate, as China's approach is based on its political and social realities, and its methods are widely used in areas other than the antitrust field. The tightening of regulations this time resulted in full-scale investigations and punishments of many platform operators in a short period of less than two years. Some consider this part of a political campaign, not mere law enforcement.[59] Certainly, there is a strong indication of state intervention in China's laws and regulations, but it is inappropriate to evaluate the timeliness thereof solely in terms of the length of time involved. The diversity and rapid development of the platform economy demands a rapid and efficient legal response. If an investigation is conducted in a reasonable period based on a fair and transparent process, and the law is applied appropriately as per the regulations, then a short time frame is desirable.

Should We Incorporate the EU's Ex Ante Regulations?

The choice between ex ante and ex post regulations in antitrust law is a matter of debate. In the period of tighter regulation, China introduced ex ante regulatory guidelines based on the EU's DMA and DSA, and the importance of these guidelines has been emphasised.[60] However, some argue that the rationale for ex ante regulation is weak, as the application of competition law takes time and delays legal action.[61] In addition, the EU's criteria for designating gatekeepers are considered rigid and lack objectivity and fairness. Bulk ex ante regulation may undermine company innovation and user interests, and many are cautious about introducing it in China.[62] EU ex ante regulation is part of an industrial policy bearing companies in other countries in mind, which differs from China's situation. Since the system and environment for applying ex ante regulation are not yet established, its introduction is not considered appropriate. The enforcement of antitrust regulation in China is linked to the political background and industrial policy, and the role of antitrust regulation in platform regulation should be fully discussed before examining the necessity and specifics of ex ante regulation. While it could be beneficial, China's specific circumstances must be considered.

From 2022 Onward: Normalised Supervisory Control Period

Overview

After 2022, the Chinese government refrained from using the phrase 'curbing the uncontrolled expansion of capital' to tighten regulations, instead emphasising 'normalisation supervision and management' (continuous regulation). In 2023, SAMR announced it would 'improve the level of normalisation supervision and management and promote the sustainable development of the platform economy', suggesting this stance would be maintained in the future.[63]

Legislative developments during this period included revisions to competition laws and regulations, such as the Anti-Monopoly Law and the Anti-Unfair Competition Law, as well as the enactment of detailed regulations to enhance the effectiveness of law enforcement and application. The authorities' regulatory goal is to ensure market stability and the responsibility of platform operators through developing and applying fair and transparent regulations. To achieve this, in addition to administrative penalties under the Anti-Monopoly Law, the authorities are promoting supervision and management at each stage of the process: ex ante (prior consultation, establishment, and implementation of compliance systems), during (administrative guidance, efficient examination, unconditional approval of business combinations), and ex post (enhanced pursuit of responsibility, monitoring of enforcement). These initiatives aim to enhance companies' voluntary awareness of compliance by adopting flexible regulatory methods and emphasising proactive prevention, while taking into account the distinctive characteristics of the platform.

Under these circumstances, the application of the Anti-Monopoly Law to platform operators declined significantly. According to the 2022 Enforcement Report, SAMR cracked down on 187 cases under the Anti-Monopoly Law, and the total amount of fines and confiscated illegal income decreased to RMB 784 million. Of these, only one case involved the abuse of a market dominant position, six the abuse of administrative power to restrict competition against platform operators, and 24 pertained to business concentration. Administrative penalties were imposed on 27 undeclared cases. The fines totalled RMB 104.1 billion.

Notably, in January 2022, CNKI, the largest platform for academic information, was fined RMB 87.6 million and ordered to cease illegal activities for the abuse of its dominant market position. It was also required to terminate its exclusive cooperation, reduce user burden, and strengthen compliance. The company was again fined RMB 50 million in 2023 for violating the Personal Information Protection Law. Furthermore, according to the 2023 'Enforcement Report', SAMR investigated 27 cases related to monopoly agreements and abuse of market dominant position, with total fines amounting to RMB 2.163 billion. In addition, in 2023, 797 business concentration cases (of which 16 were platform-related) were heard, of which 782 (more than 98%) were approved without conditions from 2022 to 2023, the application of the Anti-Monopoly Law to platform operators was restrained, and the number of crackdowns was limited.

Regarding the approval of business concentrations, the average review period was short (25.7 days), and the rate of unconditional approvals was high, indicating the efficiency and lenient attitude with which the Anti-Monopoly Law was enforced. However, as evidenced by the high fines and ongoing corrective action demands against CNKI, strict measures are being enforced for important cases. Finally, while there were no punishable platform cases in 2023, SAMR reported that it supervised and monitored the implementation of corrective measures issued in the Alibaba and Meituan cases in 2021. These details are not publicly available.

Considerations

After 2022, platform regulation shifted from being strict to flexible and stable supervision and control. Major changes in China's economic environment underlie this turnaround.[64] Stricter regulations, the Covid-19 pandemic, and the US-China trade dispute have deteriorated the performance of platform companies and led to layoffs, forcing the government to change its regulatory policies. In addition, due to tighter regulations, platform firms have developed compliance systems and initiatives, decreasing the number of cases of regulatory violations, which may have reduced the urgency of regulatory tightening.

Balance between Innovation and Discipline

The policy shift in China's Anti-Monopoly Law – inclusion and indulgence, tighter regulation, normalisation – may be criticised as a change that undermines legal stability and predictability. However, the economic environment and platform operations are changing daily, and as new issues arise, legal and regulatory stability must be maintained. It is also necessary to remain resilient by adding innovations to soft law and policy implementation methods. From this perspective, China's approach and its changes, while having top-down characteristics, are not particularly deviant actions and can be reasonably understood in the country's context.

As noted, given the close relationship between the Chinese state and platforms, platforms face the dilemma of growing in an inclusive legal environment and being increasingly regulated by authorities as their economic and social impact grows. Furthermore, the Chinese government, like other countries, relies on the multifaceted functions of giant platformers and tries to balance government control and innovation. It is also possible that the tightening of regulations was temporary and coincided with the strengthening of other laws and regulations, thus creating the illusion that antitrust regulations more significantly impacted platforms. In fact, as the Alibaba case discussed below shows, at any point, the regulations for platforms have been modestly implemented to avoid shaking the country's economic foundation.

State Regulation

In recent years, platform regulation in China has been characterised by the rapidity of investigations and disciplinary actions and the use of various means for control, including administrative guidance, prior consultation, interviews, and training sessions.[65] These regulations extend beyond mere application of the law, and decisions are made emphasising political, economic, and social impacts. As a result, effective control has been achieved in China in a shorter period than in other countries. This is partly due to the Chinese government's strong intervention regime, which is legally permissible.

Chinese government intervention has a broad and complex impact on platform regulation. Specific intervention measures have been proposed, such as the introduction of golden shares for giant platform companies[66] and establishment of a government-led antitrust regulatory compliance regime. However, whether these strong interventions are justified is debatable. The justifications include the need to respond to market failures, the enormous influence of platforms and limits of self-regulation, and need for regulation in the public interest, although these rationales are also arguable. In China, there is a risk of abuse of administrative authority and abrupt intervention that could disrupt markets and businesses, and mandatory regulation is likely to cause serious harm. However, there is also a rationale for state intervention to ensure market stability, fairness, and national security. Particularly in China, where the relationship between the state and market is close, a blanket judgment on the merits of intervention is difficult. However, as long as strong government and state capitalism are the premise, there is a risk that platform regulation could lead to excessive regulation. Therefore, it is desirable to regulate as loosely as possible, while considering the relationship between the state and market and platform characteristics.

Case Study: Alibaba and the 'Pick One from Two' Antitrust Case

The Case of Alibaba

The case has attracted worldwide attention and been the subject of numerous studies.[67] This chapter omits a detailed examination of the facts and focuses on case features and caveats. In December 2020, SAMR began investigating the Alibaba Group for allegedly abusing its dominant market position, and in April 2021, Alibaba was fined RMB 18.228 billion for 'pick one from two' in the Chinese e-commerce market. SAMR also issued an administrative guidance letter to Alibaba requiring it to strengthen compliance and take remedial measures to protect its business partners and consumers, and required it to submit an annual voluntary compliance inspection report. At this time, the Anti-Monopoly Law had not yet been amended, and the decision to impose administrative penalties was based on the guidelines.[68]

SAMR made its decision in the following three steps. First, regarding the delineation of the relevant market, the previously unclear method of delineating the two-sided platform market was analysed based on the substitutability of demand (store openers and consumers) and supply. The characteristics of the platform economy (indirect network effects) were also considered to determine the intra-China online retail platform service market.

Next, regarding whether Alibaba had a dominant market position, although Alibaba claimed the market was pluralistic, SAMR analysed Alibaba's market share, sales, price control, financial and technological strength, the degree of dependence of store operators on Alibaba, and barriers to entry by other companies, finding a dominant market position.

Finally, regarding the existence of abusive practices, SAMR proved that between 2015 and 2019, Alibaba restricted businesses on its platform from opening stores on competing platforms (e.g., JD.com and Pinduoduo), participating in other campaigns, and doing business only with Alibaba. Based on these analyses, SAMR concluded that the conduct constituted "restricting a counterparty to trade only with itself without just cause" as stipulated in Article 17, Paragraph 1, Item 4 of the former Anti-Monopoly Law, and issued an administrative sanction.

The Alibaba case is important, as it highlights the leadership role of SAMR in clarifying the platform regulatory framework (how to assess dominance and the need for regulation) and providing guidance for the application of antitrust law in this area.[69] This case marks a significant turning point in China's antitrust law and represents a new phase of government oversight and intervention against platforms, including the abuse of market dominance as well as data and security. It also served as an opportunity to reaffirm the importance of market transparency and fairness in platform operations.[70] Furthermore, regarding applying the law, this disposition can be evaluated as a logical and well-reasoned decision, consistent with international legislation, as the 'pick one from two' behaviour is prohibited in other countries.

However, there are some caveats to the administrative action in this case. At the end of 2015, JD.com alerted the authorities, accusing Alibaba of 'pick one from two' behaviour An investigation was launched but ended halfway through. It is unclear why the action was not disposed of at the time, but suddenly implemented five years later. Possibly, this was due to ambiguity in Chinese laws and regulations or a delay in authorities' decision-making process. Although the fine was huge, it was only 4% of Alibaba's previous year's sales, and thus not a fatal blow. In addition, the reason illegal income was not confiscated is not specified. It is assumed that this was the result of Alibaba's internal investigation, suspension of illegal activities, and remedial measures.[71] Regardless, this is not appropriate in terms of the principle of proportionality. No case of the harshest punishment has been ordered under China's Anti-Monopoly Law, and while not severely punished, Alibaba's situation serves as a warning and deterrent to other platforms.

Traditionally, the regulation of monopoly issues on platforms has mainly been through administrative action by SAMR, with few civil lawsuits and a limited role for the courts. However, in 2017, JD.com filed a civil lawsuit with the Beijing High Court regarding the Alibaba Group's Tmall 'pick one from two' conduct. In December 2023, the High Court recognised Tmall's illegal conduct and ordered JD.com to pay RMB 1 billion in damages.[72] In May 2024, Alibaba appealed to the Supreme Court, and while it will take some time before a final ruling is issued, the case has attracted significant public attention. With the 2022 amendments to the Anti-Monopoly Law and related regulations, anti-monopoly litigation against platforms is expected to play an important role in the future.

Implications for Alibaba's Governance

A unique and important part of Alibaba's governance structure is the partnership system.[73] This system is similar to a dual-class structure, where partners, consisting of founders, management, and selected employees, determine the company's business strategy and appoint directors, thereby controlling and maintaining a culture of control. In 2023, Alibaba underwent a major restructuring that split its main business into six companies, but the partnership system remained in place. Although this system was deficient in risk management and compliance in the wake of administrative actions, Alibaba quickly took remedial measures and strengthened its compliance system. As a result, the partnership system can be evaluated as having played an important role in supporting the multifaceted development of the company in terms of rapid decision-making, strict supervision, and stable governance.

Finally, the VIE structure of platforms including Alibaba has long been viewed as problematic at home and abroad. In its 2017 disclosure to the US SEC, Alibaba pointed out the risk of companies with VIE structures failing to file in advance with Chinese antitrust regulators. However, by 2022, 28 cases in which Alibaba and its affiliated companies received administrative sanctions for failure to file have been approved unconditionally after paying a fine of RMB 500,000. This suggests the possibility of increased risk for platformers relying on the VIE structure, and it may be necessary to re-evaluate the VIE structure and consider a different one that is legally secure. On the other hand, the fact that antitrust regulations have rendered VIE schemes subject to reporting may have the effect of providing clear guidance to companies and facilitating compliance.

Conclusion

Different countries have different legal frameworks and attitudes toward giant platformers. This chapter provides a comprehensive examination of the laws and regulations governing platformers in China, focusing on competition law. Although China's political, social, and market structures differ from those in the West, there are some similarities in terms of the legal system. The chapter touches on various related regulatory issues but focuses on presenting aspects of Chinese law that differ from the view thereof generally discussed in the West. Chinese platformers have experienced significant growth in a special institutional environment and are expected to continue to change their strategies in response to regulatory developments. Continued consideration of this topic will provide useful insights for other countries.

Notes

1 China Academy of Information and Communications Technology, *2024 World Digital Economy White Paper*. (2024, July 2).
2 'Forced to Change: Tech Giants Bow to Global Onslaught of Rules', https://www.nytimes.com/2024/03/04/technology/europe-apple-meta-google-microsoft.html?_x_tr_sl=en&_x_tr_tl=en&_x_tr_hl=en&_x_tr_pto=sc
3 In 2022, the digital economy in China surpassed US$7 trillion, accounting for 41.5% of the country's GDP. The asset value of digital platforms totalled US$2.02 trillion, representing 22.5% of the global digital platform assets, making China the second largest after the US. Information and Communications Technology, *China Digital Economy Industry Development Report* (2023).
4 'Pick one from two' refers to a practice on e-commerce and digital platforms where a business, leveraging its dominant market position, forces its partners (e.g., sellers or

suppliers) to exclusively offer their products or services on a specific platform, prohibiting them from doing so on others. This restricts business partners from engaging with competitors.

5 Price discrimination using big data refers to the practice where platforms analyse users' past purchasing history and behaviour patterns using big data to offer transactions under unfavourable conditions to specific users.

6 Sandra Marco Colino. (2022). 'The Case Against Alibaba in China and Its Wider Policy Repercussions', *Journal of Antitrust Enforcement*, 10(1), 217–229. https://doi.org/10.1093/jaenfo/jnab022.

7 Wang, X. (2023). Positioning and Measures of Platform Economic Power and Antitrust under Normalized Supervision.

8 Sun, J. (2021). 'Antitrust Regulation of Digital Platforms', *Social Sciences in China*, (05), 101–127.

9 SAMR. (2023). https://www.samr.gov.cn/zw/zfxxgk/fdzdgknr/xwxcs/art/2023/art_78e487fb7b464e79880fdc8216c08c4c.html

10 Kawashima, F. (2021). 'The Strengthening of Regulations by the Chinese Government against Platformers and the Future of Digital Innovation in China: The Case of Ant Group', Tokyo Foundation for Policy Research. (R-2021-041).

11 Zheng, W. (2023). 'The Chinese Antitrust Paradox', *University of Chicago Business Law Review*, 2(2). https://businesslawreview.uchicago.edu/print-archive/chinese-antitrust-paradox

12 Matsuo, T., & Liu, S. (2022). 'Trends in Chinese Competition Law in the Information Sector'. In S. Ishimoto, T. Matsuo, & A. Moriwaki (Eds.), *China's Digital Strategy and Law: The Current State of Chinese Information Law and the Future of the Digital Society* (pp. 129–168). Koubundou.

13 Tongshi Regulatory Penalty [2019] 3037.

14 Kawashima, F. (2020). *Legal Regulations in the Field Of E-commerce in China: Focusing on the Anti-Monopoly Law, the Anti-Unfair Competition Law, and the E-Commerce Law*. Discussion Paper Series (No. 20-J-022).

15 Kawashima, supra note 10.

16 Wang, X. (2020). 'On the Legal Regulation of "Pick One from Two" Behavior on E-commerce Platforms', *Modern Law Science*, 3(151), 12.

17 Among the typical intellectual property cases in 2023, 20 were related to data, of which 18 involved the application of the Anti-Unfair Competition Law; Su, Z., & Chen, Y. (2024, June 28). Judicial rules in data-related unfair competition: Analysis of 2023 cases in Chinese courts.

'Reexamining the Relationship Between Intellectual Property Law and Anti-Unfair Competition Law',

18 Liu, Y. (2023).

19 Jiang, L. (2021). A Study on the Legal Framework of Exclusive Transactions in Digital Platform Competition in China; Zhao, X. (2021). 'The Ternary Regulation Path and Improvement of the "Pick One from Two" Behavior on E-commerce Platforms', *Journal of Law Application*, (10), 153–166.

20 Lin, S. (2022). 'The Antitrust Regulation Logic and Development of the "Pick One from Two" Behavior on E-commerce Platforms', *Review*, (01), 490–506.

21 Zhao, supra note 19.

22 Jiang, supra note 19.

23 Creemers, R. (2021). 'Cybersecurity Law and Regulation in China: Securing the Smart State', *China Law and Society Review*, 6(2), 111–145. https://brill.com/view/journals/clsr/6/2/article-p111_001.xml; Ishimoto, S. (2022). 'National Security and Information Law'. In S. Ishimoto (Ed.), *China's Digital Strategy and Law*.

24 Creemers, R. (2021). 'Cybersecurity Law and Regulation in China: Securing the Smart State'.

25 Ma, W. (2023). China is waking up to data protection and privacy. Here's why that matters. https://www.weforum.org/agenda/2023/06/china-data-protection-privacy/
26 Calzada, I. (2022). 'Citizens' Data Privacy in China: The State of the Art of the Personal Information Protection Law (PIPL)', *Smart Cities*, 5(3), 1129–1150. https://doi.org/10.3390/smartcities5030057
27 Wu, L., Wang, W., Zhong, Y., & Zheng, X. (2022). 'A One-Year Observation of the Personal Information Protection Law', *21st Century Business Herald*. https://m.21jingji.com/article/20221102/herald/27b1efcebd37c3c5635ad39bd29065a4.html
28 Tencent.(2020). *Tencent Data Security Solutions White Paper*. https://cloud.tencent.com/developer/article/1647275
29 Liu, L. (2021). 'The Rise of Data Politics: Digital China and the World', *Studies in Comparative International Development*, 56(1), 45–67. https://doi.org/10.1007/s12116-021-09319-8
30 Donaldson, K. (2023, March 12). 'UK Set to Ban TikTok from Use on Government Devices'.
31 Zhang, T. (2024). 'PIPL vs GDPR: Key Differences and Implications for Compliance in China'. China Briefing. https://www.china-briefing.com/news/pipl-vs-gdpr-key-differences-and-implications-for-compliance-in-china/
32 Lee, S. (2023, February 22). 'Some ESG Investors Divest Tencent Shares Amid Concerns Over Chinese Censorship and Regulatory Risks', *Bloomberg*. https://www.bloomberg.co.jp/news/articles/2023-02-22/RQGNQGT1UM0W01
33 Alibaba and JD.com are supporting the enforcement of debt repayment by the courts and promoting the construction of 'smart cities' by local governments, thereby cooperating with the country's key initiatives. Couture, V., Faber, B., Gu, Y., & Liu, L. (2021). 'E-commerce Integration with Rural Areas: Evidence from China', *American Economic Review: Insights*.
34 Liu, L., supra note 29.
35 This section has been organized with reference to the following work: From 'Inclusive and Cautious' to 'Normalized Supervision and Management': The Shift in China's Platform Regulation Stance. *Perspectives on the Digital Ecosystem* (pp. 338–356). Nihon Hyoronsha.
36 Zheng, W., supra note 11.
37 Zheng, W., supra note 11.
38 Wang, X. (2024). 'A Critique of the "EU Model" in Antitrust Regulation of China's Platform Economy'.
39 Meituan 'Pick One from Two' Unfair Competition Administrative Penalty Case.
40 Bai, R. (2023). *Antitrust Enforcement Leadership and Industry Regulation Coordination in Platform Economy Supervision: Theoretical Analysis and China's Model Research on Financial and Economic Issues*, (04), 14–30.
41 Wang, X., supra note 7.
42 https://www.gov.cn/gongbao/content/2019/content_5421543.htm
43 Okano, T. (2018, November 6). 'The Rise and Prospects of Chinese Digital Companies: 2nd China Economic Research Meeting', NTT Data Institute of Management Consulting. https://npi.or.jp/publications/seminar_ce_no2_20181106.pdf
44 Wang, X. supra note 7.
45 Fukumoto, T. (2021). 'The Strengthening of Regulations by the Chinese Government against Platformers and the Future of Digital Innovation in China: The Case of Ant Group', Tokyo Foundation for Policy Research. (R-2021-041).
46 Wang, X., supra note 38.
47 Zheng, W., supra note 11.
48 Wang, X., supra note 38.
49 State Administration for Market Regulation. (2021). Decision on Administrative Penalty No. 74.

50 The announcement by SAMR regarding the decision on the antitrust review to prohibit the merger between Huya Inc. and Douyu International Holdings Limited.
51 Disposition Decision No. 65 of SAMR 2021
52 McKnight, S., Kenney, M., & Breznitz, D. (2023). 'Regulating the Platform Giants: Building and Governing China's Online Economy', *Policy & Internet*, 15(2), 243–265.
53 Kawashima, F. (2021). Strengthened Regulation of Digital Platform Operators in China: Background, Characteristics, and Outlook. Promotion Center, 'The World and Japan under the COVID-19 Shock: The Era of the Great Reset.'
54 Rong, K., Sokol, D. D., Zhou, D., & Zhu, F. (2024). *Antitrust Platform Regulation and Entrepreneurship: Evidence from China.* Working Paper, (24-039).
55 McKnight, S. et al., supra note 53.
56 Some literature points to the shift in the political dynamics of antitrust regulation toward platform companies in China as a contributing factor. Kawashima, supra note 10.
57 Zhang, Y., & Gong, S. (2023). 'A Recent Regulatory Storm in China: Theoretical Interpretation and Applicability', *Asian Review of Political Economy*, 2(1). https://doi.org/10.1007/s44216-023-00011-3
58 Thomas, Pradip Ninan, 'Platform Regulation: Exemplars, Approaches, and Solutions' (Oxford, 2023; online edn, Oxford Academic, 22 June 2023), https://doi.org/10.1093/oso/9780192887962.001.0001
59 Wang, X., supra note 38.
60 Wu Shenkuo & Hu Ran.(2021). 'The EU's New Regulatory Framework for Digital Platforms and Reflections for China: An Analysis Centered on the Proposals of the Digital Services Act and E-Government', (02), 111–120. DOI: 10.16582/j.cnki.dzzw.2021.02.010.
61 Takigawa, T. (2024). 'Issues with Mobile Ecosystems and App Store Regulation Law: Pre-Regulation vs. Antitrust Law Application'.
62 Wang, X., supra note 38.
63 People's Network.(2024, January 31). 'Enhancing the Normalization of Platform Economy Regulation', *People's Daily Online*. http://finance.people.com.cn/n1/2024/0131/c1004-40170299.html
64 Wang, X., supra note 38.
65 Sun, J. (2024). 'Public Regulation of Digital Platform's "Either-or Choice" Behavior by Anti-monopoly Law', *Law*, (2), 51–62.
66 Zou, Q. (2024). 'The Legal Basis and Institutional Construction of State Intervention in the Governance of Super Platform Companies', *Studies in Law and Business*, (1), 107–123.
67 Chen, Y. (2022). 'Antitrust Remedies: A Comparison Between the Cases Against Alibaba and Facebook'; Huandong, G. (2023). 'China's Anti-Monopoly Enforcement Campaign against Exclusionary Conduct of Two-Sided Platforms: A Case Study'.
68 SAMR Penalty Letter [2021] No. 28.
69 Colino, S. M. (2022). 'The Case Against Alibaba in China and Its Wider Policy Repercussions', *Journal of Antitrust Enforcement*, 10(1), 217–229. https://doi.org/10.1093/jaenfo/jnab022.
70 Huandong, supra note 67.
71 Kawashima, supra note 10.
72 Zheng, S. (2023, December 29). 'JD Wins 100 Million Yuan in Damages in Antimonopoly Case Against Alibaba'.
73 For more details, please refer to Lu, X. (2021). 'Creating a Classified Stock Structure in China: An Analysis of Alibaba's "Partnership Structure"', *Interdisciplinary Journal of Economics and Business Law*, 10(3), 27–52.

6 Addendum: Excessive Patenting in Big Pharma: Should This Strategy Be Regulated by Competition Law as Big Tech Targets Healthcare?

Naoko Mariyama

Introduction

Intellectual property rights provide incentives for inventing by giving exclusive rights to inventors. Business leaders have emphasised that patent protection is critical for attracting the capital necessary to fund high-risk investments.[1] Research and development (R&D) is sometimes very costly, and many projects fail before they even get off the ground. Patents reward businesses that take risks by giving them exclusive rights for a certain period of time. Patent protection results in high expenses in the short term, but in the long run the profits from such protection makes it possible for a company to invest in and invent new products that consumers need.

However, does a patent always promote invention? Some companies file a large number of patent applications and obtain many patents as a way to set up barriers to competition. Some of these patents do not differ from existing ones. When patents work as entry barriers, the patentee may profit from their dominant position created through excessive patenting. If a patent procedure is not used for its intended purpose, firms are essentially committing an abuse of procedure to exclude competition.[2] If companies are allowed to create barriers to entry through bogus patents and gain monopoly profits, then they are not encouraging high-risk new inventions, but rather squeezing out profits from existing inventions. It may make more sense, from a business perspective, to employ such a patent strategy rather than focus on innovation. In a situation in which such practices are rife, patents do not provide an incentive to innovate.[3]

There are clusters of improvement patents in nearly all industries.[4] Excessive patenting, though, can be especially problematic in technology-intensive industries, including the information technology (IT) industry. However, research has revealed that this particular strategy is endemic to the pharmaceutical industry.[5] Indeed, technology giants have already invaded the healthcare sector,[6] and this problem could also become an issue in the tech industry in the near future.

Simply put, excessive patenting can harm competition. In the US, Congress has introduced bills to address this patent abuse.[7] However, it remains to be seen whether these bills will actually solve the issue. Should we regulate excessive patenting through competition law, and can current competition laws deal with such antitrust issues? Do current competition law regulations need to be modernised?

DOI: 10.4324/9781003489542-6

Intellectual Property Laws and Innovation

Some argue that the US patent system has weakened the ability of companies to protect their inventions.[8] Specifically, it has been said that while the US is still strong on the aspect of intellectual property creation, it remains weak in terms of the strength of patent rights.[9]

Given that 46% of litigated patents are held to be invalid,[10] it may seem apparent that patent rights are not so strong. The United States Patent and Trademark Office (USPTO) actually encourages the granting of patents of doubtful quality through an incentive system that rewards examiners for allowing but not rejecting applications.[11] The USPTO examination process takes nearly three years on average, but due to a shortage of personnel,[12] a patent examiner spends only 18 hours per application on average.[13] It follows that many patents issued by the USPTO are of questionable validity and uncertain scope or are simply probabilistic.[14] Some would argue that excessive invalidation is sapping the strength of the patent system and innovation.[15] However, if patents are of questionable validity, invalidating those patent rights would not necessarily hinder innovation.

Big Tech companies benefit from the weak strength of IP enforcement. They abuse the patent system to eliminate competitors, and stifle innovation by preying on inventors and small businesses.[16] They have built knockoff products and launched endless challenges to start-ups, small businesses, and inventors that often do not have the resources to pursue expensive and time-consuming litigation.[17] As a result, smaller companies may be forced to spend tens of millions of dollars on protracted litigation to protect past inventions, instead of investing in R&D.[18]

To fix the problem of stealing patents from smaller rivals, Congress has introduced a bipartisan bill called the PREVAIL Act.[19] Big Pharma and opponents of Big Tech have expressed support for the bill and contend that strong patents catalyse innovation. On the other hand, opponents of this bill have argued that it would raise drug prices by taking away the last pathway to challenging erroneously-granted patents that block cheaper competitors' products from entering the market.[20] At present, Big Tech and Big Pharma seem to have opposing views on the patent system.

Nevertheless, overprotecting intellectual property is as harmful as under-protecting it.[21] Both excessive patenting and stealing patents from smaller companies are patent strategies adopted by big companies to maintain and strengthen their dominant positions. These strategies consist of abuse of the patent system and ultimately stymie innovation. In fact, companies often use a variety of patent strategies,[22] and it is difficult for the authorities to cope with these changing approaches.[23] Among these strategies is excessive patenting, which will be discussed in this chapter.

Intellectual property laws have often undermined rather than promoted innovation by granting intellectual property holders rights far beyond what is necessary to create appropriate incentives to innovate.[24] As a result, these laws have often increased the cost of innovation.[25]

A patent at issue in a litigation may or may not be valid, and may or may not be infringed.[26] An invalidated patent does not carry with it the ability to exclude others from using the protected process or product.[27] Even a valid patent confers no right to exclude products or processes that do not actually infringe.[28] Patents are in a sense probabilistic, rather than ironclad; they grant their holders a potential, but not a certain, right to exclude.[29]

Under current law, a patent owner can game the regulatory system by obtaining multiple patents that are virtually indistinguishable from each other.[30] By increasing the number of weak patents, patent owners are able to increase entry costs for competitors.[31] The overwhelming majority of litigated patents in the pharmaceutical industry are secondary patents that claim changes in formulation, dissolution profiles, new uses and the like.[32] These patents are aimed at deterring generic entry and in many cases, they are from the same family and are often obvious variants of each other.[33] Even if generic manufacturers believe that a brand manufacture's patents are invalid, or that their own patents do not infringe the brands' patents, they tend to hesitate when it comes to challenging the brand manufacture's patents to enter the market, since patent lawsuits expend a great deal of time and money.

Overall, the current situation is harming innovation.[34] Rather than creating new medicines, drug companies are focusing their time and efforts on extending the patent life of old products.[35] This is not the innovation one would hope for. The greatest creativity at companies should be found in the laboratory, not in the legal department.[36] The intellectual property system is designed to benefit not only inventors but society as a whole; it gives inventors a period of exclusivity in exchange for forcing those who benefit to disclose their inventions so that competitors can use them.[37]

It is well-established case law that the possession of valid patents does not give the patentee any exemption from antitrust law beyond the limits of the patent monopoly.[38] Both patent and antitrust laws aim to encourage innovation and competition.[39] Excessive patenting, including dubious patents, may unfairly extend the duration of exclusive patent rights and extend the limits of a patent monopoly. In such a situation, it seems that the strategy should be regulated by competition law.

The US Seventh Circuit Case on Humira

In one particular case in the US,[40] the focus was on this kind of patent strategy. Specifically, it concerned a drug called Humira, which is a biological drug used to treat a variety of autoimmune disorders ranging from Crohn's disease to plaque psoriasis.[41] Humira is one of the world's best-selling and most profitable drugs.[42]

AbbVie, the owner of Humira, filed 247 patent applications for Humira in the US, with the aim of delaying competition, and obtained 132 patents. While the basic US patent for Humira expired at the end of 2016, nearly 50% of the patents (122 of 247) were filed by AbbVie from 2014 onwards, more than 20 years after initial scientific research began, and more than a decade after the product started being sold.[43] AbbVie obtained additional patents related to the drug, such as patents for manufacturing and administration.[44] These patents are called secondary patents, as opposed to basic or primary patents, which protect a novel chemical entity. Drug companies are more likely to win on primary active-ingredient patents (92%) than on secondary patents (32%).[45]

Since launching Humira in 2003, AbbVie has raised the drug's price 27 times, including by nearly 30% in one 10-month period.[46] The price of a 40-milligram syringe of Humira has increased by 470% since the drug's launch.[47] Over two-thirds of Humira's US sales have come since the March 2016 expiration of its primary patents.[48]

The plaintiff, which in this case consisted of welfare-benefit plans that pay for Humira on behalf of covered beneficiaries, alleged that AbbVie maintained its monopoly by obtaining and asserting swaths of invalid, unenforceable, or non-infringing patents without regard for their merits.[49] Such practices allegedly delayed entry of biosimilars – as copies of pharmaceutical drugs are called – by repeatedly and aggressively asserting a patent thicket during a lengthy, detailed regulatory process and subsequent infringement litigation.[50]

A patent thicket is defined as "an overlapping set of patent rights requiring that those seeking to commercialise new technology obtain licenses from multiple patentees".[51] Patent thickets, according to this definition, involve multiple parties having overlapping patent rights on a single product, which requires competitors to negotiate licenses with each other to bring the product to market.[52] In contrast, the patent thicket asserted in this case involved a single party creating a large web of patents to deter or delay the entry of competitors into the market, so that the firm did not need to coordinate or negotiate with others, given that competitors are prevented from entering the market.[53]

The plaintiff argued that AbbVie violated US antitrust law by obtaining too many patents that were weak and subject to challenge, thereby establishing a 'patent thicket'.[54] In fact, some of AbbVie's patents were invalidated during proceedings before the USPTO.[55] However, the Seventh Circuit Court rejected the argument. The Court held that nothing is wrong with having a large number of patents,[56] and the plaintiffs did not prove that all 132 patents were invalid.[57] Even if patents are weak, as the plaintiffs insisted, weak patents are valid.[58]

The Court continued that while objectively baseless petitions to the government can violate antitrust laws if they smother competition, that AbbVie's patent applications could not be called baseless, because 132 patents had actually been issued.[59]

Patent application is considered a petition to the government.[60] According to the Noerr-Pennington doctrine, which is rooted in the First Amendment of the US Constitution, petitioning activities are immune from antitrust liability. Such immunity can be withheld, and the application of the Sherman Act would be justified when petitioning activity "ostensibly directed toward influencing governmental action … is a mere sham to cover … an attempt to interfere directly with the business relationships of a competitor"[61] through the "use [of] the governmental process – as opposed to the outcome of that process – as an anticompetitive weapon".[62]

With regard to the Noerr-Peninngton doctrine, the Court held that the plaintiffs in this case "express[ed] concern about the successful outcome of the petitioning, not about the costs imposed by the process of petitioning. Patent applications, successful or not, do not impose costs on rivals; only issued patents do so".[63]

While it is true that patent application processes do not prevent the entry of competitors, in this case, it seems that what prevented biosimilars from entering the market was not the innovation contained in the patents, but the costly and time-consuming process of invalidating the many patents that made up the patent thicket.

Thus, what was at issue in this case were the numerous patent applications and the resulting patents. In relation to repeated patent applications, which means repeated petitions to the government, the Second, Third, Fourth, Ninth, and Tenth Circuit courts hold that if a series of petitions demonstrate a pattern of filings made solely to inflict harm through a burdensome process, without consideration of the merits of or interest in the requested relief, antitrust immunity may be lost under the sham exception.[64] As a result, these courts hold that the overall pattern of filings can qualify as a sham and would therefore be subject to competition law, even if some petitions among them are objectively reasonable.[65]

Nevertheless, it should be noted that other circuit courts have a different view of this matter. The First and Seventh Circuit courts have held that every petition is subject to the same test, in that it must be determined (1) whether it was objectively baseless, and, if so, (2) whether the subjective intent of the petitioning was to harm a rival.[66] Therefore, only objectively baseless petitions can give rise to antitrust liability, and Noerr-Pennington shields a pattern of petitions that are objectively reasonable.[67] As a result, a series of petitions may be immune from antitrust liability, even if they succeed in barring the entry of a competitor or raising a rival's costs, so long as each petition is considered objectively reasonable.[68]

Although the Supreme Court has not resolved the circuit split,[69] considering the definition of excessive patenting according to the opinions of the Second, Third, Fourth, Ninth, and Tenth Circuit courts, the repetitive patent filing in this case may be considered as an act of engaging in sham petitions and thus be subject to competition law.

In the Humira case, the Seventh Circuit held that AbbVie's patent strategy of creating a patent thicket to prevent biosimilar entry did not infringe on competition law. The Court held that there was nothing wrong with having a large number of patents. Is that really the case, though?

Excessive patenting is widespread in the US pharma sector. On average, there are 74 granted patents for each of America's ten top-selling drugs, which has effectively provided major drug makers with a substantial advantage in keeping generic and biosimilar competitors off the market.[70] According to one study, 78% of the drugs associated with new patents were not new drugs coming on to the market, but existing drugs.[71] Out of the 106 top-selling drugs between 2005 and 2014, more than 70% had extended their protection cliff at least once and more than 50% had extended it more than once.[72] From this, we can reasonably conclude that stifling competition through excessive patenting has become the norm in the pharmaceutical industry.[73]

Excessive patenting is not just problematic in the US, however. It is also problematic in Europe.

Case of Teva EU and European Commission

The European Commission's view of the misuse of the patent system is as follows: Competition authorities have a role to play in such scenarios to ensure that incentives to innovate are not distorted and that healthcare systems are not worse off as a result of companies unduly obstructing competition to protect their revenues.[74] It is also important for generic and biosimilar manufacturers to be able to anticipate when patents and other exclusivities protecting an originator drug expire so that they can then enter and compete on the market.[75]

The European Commission report on the pharmaceutical sector which was published in 2024 listed the misuse of the patent system and abusive litigation to prolong patent exclusivity as anticompetitive practices that have harmed innovation and prices.[76]

In addition to the Commission's reports, there has been an exemplary case on excessive patenting.[77] The European Commission sent a statement objection to the pharmaceutical company Teva in 2022, and an oral hearing was held in 2023.[78] Teva's blockbuster medicine, Copaxone, is widely used for the treatment of multiple sclerosis and contains the active pharmaceutical ingredient glatiramer acetate, over which Teva held a basic patent until 2015.[79]

The Commission preliminarily found that Teva abused its dominant position in the markets for glatiramer acetate in Belgium, Czechia, Germany, Italy, the Netherlands, Poland, and Spain.[80] In particular, the Commission considered that Teva had artificially extended glatiramer acetate patent protection by filing and withdrawing secondary patent applications, thereby forcing its competitors to file new lengthy legal challenges each time.[81] In this way, patent strategies such as excessive patenting may be subject to competition law in Europe.

Monopolists tend to want to keep their monopolies by resorting to measures that will keep new entrants out. Firms under competitive pressure from actual or potential competition, on the other hand, are less complacent and know that inventing a new product is their best strategy for maintaining and increasing their market share.[82] Since the patent system is based on the idea of dynamic competition, once the procurement of patents by a dominant firm becomes a means for extending a monopoly and harming competition, the authorities must intervene.[83]

The existence of a patent cannot, as such, be regarded as an insurmountable barrier.[84] Furthermore, obtaining numerous patents to prevent competition cannot be illegal in itself. However, clustering patents only for the purpose of excluding competition and not for safeguarding a viable commercial development that is a result of a company's own innovation is not in line with the underlying objectives of patent systems and is thus an anticompetitive act. Such practices may have a significant exclusionary effect, so they should be regulated by competition law. However, in what circumstances would such a strategy be unlawful, and how should it be regulated? Within this context it is apposite to consider these criteria by referring to the Actavis case heard by the Supreme Court of the United States.

The Actavis Case

The Actavis case[85] involved a settlement agreement in a patent infringement lawsuit, known as reverse payment or pay-for-delay. In this kind of agreement, a 'brand' pharmaceutical company pays generic manufacturers a large amount of money. In return, the generic manufacturer delays its entry into the market.

The circuit courts had been divided in their views on such agreements. Some courts applied the scope of the patent test, which holds that as long as the anticompetitive effect of the settlement agreement falls within the exclusionary scope of the patent, the settlement is immune from antitrust attacks.[86] Other courts had held that this type of agreement is presumptively unlawful.[87] In the absence of proof of other offsetting considerations, it is logical to conclude that the quid pro quo for the payment is an agreement by the generic to defer entry beyond the date that represented an otherwise reasonable litigation compromise.[88]

With the circuit courts thus divided in their opinions about such agreements, the Supreme Court ruled as follows: First, the Court rejected the scope of the patent test because the patent in the litigation may or may not have been valid, and the settlement might have had significant adverse effects on competition.[89] In citing case law, the Court stated that the improper use of [a patent] monopoly, is 'invalid' under the antitrust laws,[90] and that "[there is] public interest in granting patent monopolies only to the extent that the public is given a novel and useful invention in consideration for its grant".[91]

Furthermore, the Court held that:

> a reverse payment, where large and unjustified, can bring with it the risk of significant anticompetitive effects; one who makes such a payment may be unable to explain and to justify it; such a firm or individual may well possess market power derived from the patent; a court, by examining the size of the payment, may well be able to assess its likely anticompetitive effects along with its potential justifications without litigating the validity of the patent.[92]

The Court presented justifications for the pay-for-delay agreement, which included avoiding litigation costs and fair value for services by generic manufactures.[93] A pay-for-delay agreement with such justifications would not bring about an anticompetitive effect.[94]

Following this Supreme Court decision, prominent scholars have presented criteria for evaluating pay-for-delay agreements.[95] The agreements subject to these criteria involve the following:

1 A large payment, in some form, from the patentee to the alleged infringer; and
2 A requirement that the alleged infringer refrain from competing for some period of time and, in some respects, using, the patented technology.[96]

The criteria themselves are as follows: The plaintiff must establish that (a) the claimed infringer has agreed to abstain, in some respects, from competing using the patented technology for a period of time, and (b) that there was an otherwise unexplained payment from the patent holder to the claimed infringer.[97] The unexplained payment is shown by any consideration flowing from the patentee to the claimed infringer minus the patent holder's avoided litigation costs and payment of the value of goods, services or other consideration provided by the claimed infringer to the patent holder.[98] If these criteria are met, the payment is considered to have been issued for a delay.[99]

Concerning the allocation of the burden of proof, the plaintiff must establish the restriction of competition, and the payment from the patentee to the alleged infringer must be larger than the patentee's avoided litigation cost.[100] Then the defendants should prove that the payment was for valuable services rather than for a delay, because, after all, the defendants must have the relevant evidence to support their deal.[101]

How to Regulate Excessive Patenting

Excessive patenting strategies need to be regulated in certain cases. If companies are allowed to file any patent application, or any number of them, without any restrictions, companies may not use their resources productively, and may instead leverage them for patent procedures. The General Court of the EU has held that "misuse of the patent system potentially reduces the incentive to engage in innovation, since it enables the company in a dominant position to maintain its exclusivity beyond the period envisaged by the legislator".[102]

A patent monopoly should be given to the extent that the public is provided with a novel and useful invention. Allowing excessive patenting discourages innovation. Creating a new invention is a costly, time-consuming and uncertain business. At the same time, obtaining secondary patents for successful innovations and extending their marketing exclusivity is a less costly and more certain way to secure profits. It is thus a rational choice for companies to adopt an excessive patenting strategy. This strategy uses a costly and time-consuming patent invalidating process rather than the content of new patents to restrict competition. As such, it should be subject to competition law because it can unfairly restrict competition, and the harm caused by the strategy can be substantial. Competition law should apply to patent thickets or clusters in which there is clear circumstantial evidence that intellectual property rights have been used beyond their purpose at the expense of competition (i.e., that they were clearly not used to reward innovation but to restrict competition).[103]

How do we regulate this strategy? In the Actavis case, the US Supreme Court conceded that unjustified anticompetitive harm could be brought about by the pay-for-delay agreement. Excessive patenting may also cause unjustified anticompetitive harm. Patent laws aim to encourage innovation and benefit the public through such activities. Even if a patentee files many patent applications, such patent filings should not be subject to competition law if these patents would in fact benefit the public. On the other hand, if patents do not provide any benefit to the public, it can be concluded that they serve only to prevent the entry of generic brands.

Therefore, as in the Actavis case criteria, the plaintiff showed that the strategy restricts competition and does not have any added benefit for the public. The defendant could refute this claim by showing that the patents have added benefit to the public. If the patents do not provide any added benefits to the public, the strategy infringes upon competition law.

Note: This work was supported by the JSPS International Joint Research Programme (JRP-LEAD with UKRI) Grant Number JPJSJRP 20211703.

Notes

1 Federal Trade Commission, 'To Promote Innovation: The Proper Balance of Competition and Patent Law and Policy' (October. 2003) Ch. 3, 1.

2 Lars Kjφlbye, 'Article 82 as Remedy to Patent System Imperfections: Fighting Fire with Fire?' (2009) *World Competition*, 32, 163, 183

3 Olga Gurgula, 'Strategic Patenting by Pharmaceutical Companies – Should Competition Law Intervene?' (2020) 51 IIC Int Rev Ind Prop Copyr Law 1062, 1064 ; Robin Feldman, 'May Your Drug Price Be Evergreen' (2018) *Journal of Law and the Biosciences,* 5, 590, 640.

4 Uri Y. Hacohen, 'Evergreening at-Risk', (2020) *Harvard Journal of Law & Technology*, 33, 480, 488.

5 *Feldman* (n 3) 639.

6 Laura Cooper, 'Tech Giants' Health-Care Moves Attract PE Attention; Bain Study Says Technology Giants May Create Opportunities in Health-Care Space' *WSJ Pro. Private Equity* (New York Apr 18, 2018), https://www.wsj.com/articles/tech-giants-health-care-moves-attract-pe-attention-1524052800

7 Dick Durbin and Lina M. Khan, 'Senate, FTC Cracking Down on Pharma Patent Shenanigans, Reporting From the Frontiers of Health and Medicine', STAT (2 July 2024), https://www.statnews.com/2024/07/02/reduce-healthcare-costs-via-patent-reform-ftc-lina-khan-senator-dick-durbin/

8 Rana Foroohar, 'Big Tech vs Big Pharma: The Battle over US Patent Protection', FT.com (16 October 2017), https://www.ft.com/content/6c5b2cca-ae8b-11e7-beba-5521c713abf4#:~:text=The%20law%20established%20a%20non-court

9 Rana Foroohar, 'Big Tech vs Big Pharma'.

10 Mark A. Lemley and Carl Shapiro, 'Probabilistic Patents' (2005) *Journal of Economic Perspectives*, 19, 75, 80.

11 Mark A. Lemley and Carl Shapiro, 'Probabilistic Patents', 79.

12 *Hacohen* (n 4) 492.

13 *Hacohen* (n 4) 492.

14 *Hacohen* (n 4) 493.

15 *Foroohar* (n 8).

16 Chris Borges and Alexander Kersten, 'New Efforts to Promote U.S. Innovation: The PERA and PREVAIL Act in Context', CSIS (11 December 2023), https://www.csis.org/analysis/new-efforts-promote-us-innovation-pera-and-prevail-act-context

17 *Foroohar* (n 8); Borges and Kersten (n 16).

18 Chuck Hong, 'Big Tech's Abuse of the Patent System Must End—Take It From Me, I've Fought Google Over IP for Years' (10 August 2024) *Fortune.com*, https://fortune.com/2024/08/09/big-tech-patent-system-netlist-google-prevail-act-uspto-ptab-aia-innovation/?utm_source=search&utm_medium=suggested_search&utm_campaign=search_link_clicks

19 Andrei Iancu and David J. Kappos, 'Big Tech Wants to Keep Stealing Patents—So It's Going to War with Big Pharma' (28 August 2024) *Fortune.com*, https://fortune.com/2024/08/28/big-tech-patent-war-big-pharma-congress-politics/

20 I-MAK, 'Apr 2024: Senators Could Hand Pharma a Big Win with the PREVAIL Act,' (9 May 2024), https://www.i-mak.org/2024/05/09/apr-2024-senators-could-hand-pharma-a-big-win-with-the-prevail-act/
21 *White v Samsung Electronics American Inc*, 989 F 2d 1532, 1533 (9th Cir 1993) (Kozinski J, dissenting).
22 *Kjφlbye* (n 2) 179
23 *Kjφlbye* (n 2) 179.
24 Herbert Hovenkamp, 'Antitrust and Innovation: Where We Are and Where We Should Be Going' (2011) *Antitrust Law J.*, 77, 749.
25 Herbert Hovenkamp, 'Antitrust and Innovation'.
26 *FTC v Actavis, Inc*, 570 US 136, 147 (2013).
27 *FTC v Actavis, Inc*, 570 US 136, 147 (2013).
28 *FTC v Actavis, Inc*, 570 US 136, 147 (2013).
29 *In re Cipro Cases I & II*, 61 Cal 4th 116, 143 (Cal 2015).
30 Mark A Lemley and S. Sean Tu, 'What Litigators Can Teach the Patent Office About Pharmaceutical Patents' (2022) *Washington University Law Rev,* 99, 1673, 77.
31 Mark A Lemley and S. Sean Tu, 'What Litigators Can Teach the Patent Office About Pharmaceutical Patents'.
32 Mark A Lemley and S. Sean Tu, 'What Litigators Can Teach the Patent Office About Pharmaceutical Patents', 1691.
33 Mark A Lemley and S. Sean Tu, 'What Litigators Can Teach the Patent Office About Pharmaceutical Patents', 1708.
34 *Feldman* (n 3) 617.
35 *Feldman* (n 3) 617.
36 *Feldman* (n 3) 617.
37 *Feldman* (n 3) 639.
38 *United States v Singer Mfg Co,* 374 US 174, 196-97 (1963).
39 *Atari Games Corp v Nintendo of America Inc*, 897 F 2d 1572, 1575 (Fed Cir 1990).
40 *Mayor & City Council of Baltimore v AbbVie Inc,* 42 F 4th 709 (7th Cir 2022).
41 *In re Humira (Adalimumab) Antitrust Litigation,* 465 F Supp 3d 811, 820 (ND Ill 2020).
42 *Mayor & City Council of Baltimore v AbbVie Inc*, 42 F 4th 711 (7th Cir 2022).
43 I-MAK, 'Overpatented, Overpriced Special Edition: Humira' (September 2021) 4, https://www.i-mak.org/wp-content/uploads/2021/09/i-mak.humira.report.3.final-REVISED-2021-09-22.pdf
44 *Mayor & City Council of Baltimore v AbbVie Inc*, 42 F 4th 711 (7th Cir 2022).
45 C. Scott Hemphill and Bhaven Sampat, 'Drug Patents at the Supreme Court' (2013) *Science*, 339, 1386, 1387.
46 Staff Report Committee on Oversight and Reform, U.S. House of Representatives, 'Drug Pricing Investigation AbbVie-Humira and Imbruvica', (May 2021) Executive Summary, i, https://oversightdemocrats.house.gov/sites/evo-subsites/democrats-oversight.house.gov/files/Committee%20on%20Oversight%20and%20Reform%20-%20AbbVie%20Staff%20Report.pdf
47 Staff Report Committee on Oversight and Reform.
48 *I-MAK*, (n 43).
49 *In re Humira (Adalimumab) Antitrust Litigation*, 465 F Supp 3d 811, 827 (N D Ill 2020).
50 *In re Humira (Adalimumab) Antitrust Litigation.*
51 Carl Shapiro, 'Navigating the Patent Thicket: Cross Licenses Patent Pools, and Standard Setting' (2011), *Innovation Policy and the Economy*, 119.
52 Michael A Carrier and S. Sean Tu, 'Why Pharmaceutical Patent Thickets Are Unique' (2024) *Texas Intellectual Property Law Journal*, 32, 79, 81.
53 Michael A Carrier and S. Sean Tu, 'Why Pharmaceutical Patent Thickets Are Unique'.
54 *Mayor & City Council of Baltimore v AbbVie Inc.*, 42 F 4th 709, 712 (7th Cir 2022).
55 *Mayor & City Council of Baltimore v AbbVie Inc.*

56 *Mayor & City Council of Baltimore v AbbVie Inc.*
57 *Mayor & City Council of Baltimore v AbbVie Inc.*, 713.
58 *Mayor & City Council of Baltimore v AbbVie Inc.*, 713.
59 *Mayor & City Council of Baltimore v AbbVie Inc.*, 713.
60 Lisa Orucevic, 'A Machete for the Patent Thicket: Using Noerr-Pennington Doctrine's Sham Exception to Challenge Abusive Patent Tactics by Pharmaceutical Companies' (2022) *Vanderbilt Law Rev.*, 75, 277.
61 *Eastern Rail Road Presidents Conference v Noerr Motors*, 365 US 127, 144, 81 S Ct 523, 533 (1961).
62 *Professional Real Estate Investors, Inc v Columbia Pictures Industries, Inc*, 508 US 49, 60–61, 113 S Ct 1920, 1928 (1993).
63 *Mayor & City Council of Baltimore v AbbVie Inc*, 42 F 4th 709, 714 (7th Cir 2022).
64 Dylan Carson and Scott Russell, 'Circuits Reinforce Split over When Noerr-Pennington Shields Serial Litigants' (February 2021) The Antitrust Source 2, 6, <https://www.americanbar.org/content/dam/aba/publishing/antitrust-magazine-online/2021/feb-2021/atsource-feb2021-carson.pdf.> accessed 4 October 2024.
65 Dylan Carson and Scott Russell, 'Circuits Reinforce Split over When Noerr-Pennington Shields Serial Litigants', 2.
66 Dylan Carson and Scott Russell, 'Circuits Reinforce Split over When Noerr-Pennington Shields Serial Litigants', 2.
67 Dylan Carson and Scott Russell, 'Circuits Reinforce Split over When Noerr-Pennington Shields Serial Litigants', 2.
68 Dylan Carson and Scott Russell, 'Circuits Reinforce Split over When Noerr-Pennington Shields Serial Litigants', 2.
69 Dylan Carson and Scott Russell, 'Circuits Reinforce Split over When Noerr-Pennington Shields Serial Litigants', 14.
70 I-MAK, 'Overpatented, Overpriced – Curbing Patent Abuse: Tackling the Root of the Drug Pricing Crisis' (September 2022) 7, https://www.i-mak.org/wp-content/uploads/2022/09/Overpatented-Overpriced-2022-FINAL.pdf
71 *Feldman* (n 3) 590.
72 *Feldman* (n 3), 638.
73 *Feldman* (n 3), 638.
74 European Commission, Directorate-General for Competition, 'Update on Competition Enforcement in the Pharmaceutical Sector (2018–2022): European Competition Authorities Working Together for Affordable and Innovative Medicines – Report from the Commission to the Council and the European Parliament' (2024) 17, https://data.europa.eu/doi/10.2763/427709
75 European Commission, 'Update on Competition Enforcement in the Pharmaceutical Sector'.
76 European Commission, Press Release 'Commission Report Finds Active Competition Enforcement Continues to Contribute to Affordable and Innovative Medicines' (26 January 2024), https://ec.europa.eu/commission/presscorner/detail/en/ip_24_413
77 European Commission, Press Release, 'Antitrust: Commission Sends Statement of Objections to Teva Over Misuse of the Patent System and Disparagement of Rival Multiple Sclerosis Medicine' (10 October 2022), https://ec.europa.eu/commission/presscorner/detail/en/IP_22_6062
78 Case AT 40588 – *Teva Copaxone*, https://competition-cases.ec.europa.eu/cases/AT.40588
79 European Commission, Press Release, 'Antitrust: Commission Sends Statement of Objections to Teva Over Misuse of the Patent System and Disparagement of Rival Multiple Sclerosis Medicine' (10 October 2022), https://ec.europa.eu/commission/presscorner/detail/en/IP_22_6062
80 European Commission, Press Release, 'Antitrust'.

81 European Commission, Press Release, 'Antitrust'. With regard to this case, an interim injunction was imposed on Teva by the District Court of Munich in February 2020 (Julia Molestina, 'European Commission Investigation into Teva's Potential Abuse of Dominance – Misuse of Patent Procedures and Disparagement' [20 December 2022] Kluwer Competition Law Blog, https://competitionlawblog.kluwercompetitionlaw.com/2022/12/20/european-commission-investigation-into-tevas-potential-abuse-of-dominance-misuse-of-patent-procedures-and-disparagement/

82 Philip Lowe, 'Competition and Innovation Policy' *GCP: The Online Magazine for Global Competition Policy* (July 2008) 3, https://competitionpolicyinternational.com/assets/0d358061e11f2708ad9d62634c6c40ad/Lowe,%20GCP%20Jul-08(1).pdf

83 *Gurgula* (n 3) 1081.

84 See C-591/16 P, EU:C:2021:243, *Lundbeck v Commission,* (25 March 2021) para 38 and 58–59.

85 *FTC v Actavis, Inc*, 570 US 136.

86 See *FTC v Watson Pharmaceuticals, Inc*, 677 F 3d 1298, 1312 (2012); *In re Ciprofloxacin Hydrochloride Antitrust Litigation*, 544 F 3d 1323, 1332–1337 (Fed Cir 2008); *In re Tamoxifen Citrate Antitrust Litigation*, 466 F 3d 187, 212–213 (2d Cir 2006).

87 *In re K-Dur Antitrust Litigation*, 686 F 3d 197 (3d Cir 2012).

88 *In re K-Dur Antitrust Litigation*, 218.

89 *FTC v Actavis, Inc*, 570 US 136, 147–148.

90 *FTC v Actavis, Inc*, 570 US 136, 148, citing *United States v Line Material Co*, 333 US 287, 310 (1948).

91 *FTC v Actavis, Inc*, 570 US 136, 149, citing *United States v Singer Mfg Co*, 374 US 174, 199 (1963).

92 *FTC v Actavis, Inc*, 570 US 136, 158.

93 *FTC v Actavis, Inc*, 156.

94 *FTC v Actavis, Inc*, 156.

95 Aaron Edlin and others, 'Activating Actavis' (Fall 2013) *Antitrust Magazine* 16.

96 Aaron Edlin and others, 'Activating Actavis' (Fall 2013) *Antitrust Magazine* 16.

97 Aaron Edlin and others, 'Activating Actavis' (Fall 2013) *Antitrust Magazine*, 17–18.

98 Aaron Edlin and others, 'Activating Actavis' (Fall 2013) *Antitrust Magazine*, 18.

99 Aaron Edlin and others, 'Activating Actavis' (Fall 2013) *Antitrust Magazine*, 18.

100 Aaron Edlin and others, 'Activating Actavis' (Fall 2013) *Antitrust Magazine*, 18.

101 Aaron Edlin and others, 'Activating Actavis' (Fall 2013) *Antitrust Magazine*, 18.

102 Case T-321/05, *AstraZeneca v Commission* (1 July 2010) para 367.

103 Eric Morgan de Rivery and others, 'Lisbon Conference – Panel IV – Intellectual Property and Competition – Complementary Policies? The Case of the Software and Pharmaceutical Industries (15 January 2010)', https://www.concurrences.com/en/review/issues/no-2-2010/conferences/lisbon-conference-panel-iv-intellectual-property-and-competition-complementary-31078

7 Conclusion

Ruth Taplin

The analysis was made of the future of Competition Law in the regions assessed in relation to modernising to address new challenges brought about by the expansion of digital technology and the anti-competitive nature of the gatekeeper role of tech giants on their digital platforms. Successful new regulation in the regions addressed have shown the complexities of conceiving regulation that maintains a fair and balanced marketplace which allows tech giants to act as important gatekeepers that maintain security practices which do not facilitate cyberattack and content misinformation, while opening its digital platforms to other App providers in safety and invention. This is the essential conundrum which is being resolved at different levels and speeds throughout the regions explored in this book. The European Commission led by Margrethe Vestager is the most aggressive in curtailing Big Tech dominance through opening access to digital platforms without excessive fees to other App providers such as rival creators, SME companies, consumers, and makers of generic products. She has tried to stop illegal practices of self-preferencing as described in Chapter 1.

The Future

The European Union has been outstanding in its efforts to stop the worst anti-monopoly breaches, infringement, and practices by tech giants largely due to the efforts of titans of tech regulation Margrethe Vestager and the former European Commissioner for Internal Markets, Thierry Breton. The latter, who oversaw extensive new social media regulations under the Digital Services Act (DSA) said in the middle of September 2024 that he would resign immediately.

The former who is the top European Commission antitrust official who introduced Digital Markets Act (DMA) competition rules stepped down in late 2024 and was succeded by Teresa Ribera Rodriguez who was a Spanish official. Breton, successfully pressured tech companies to be transparent in relation to how they recommend content to users and mitigate risks posed by disinformation, actions which were codified with the adoption of the DSA in 2022. In the US this protection against disinformation has recently been challenged by Mark Zuckerberg, CEO of Meta, who fell in line after pressure from Elon Musk and Donald Trump to stop having internal experts take down objectionable content, while encouraging users

DOI: 10.4324/9781003489542-7

to be their own internal regulators of content. Breton recently berated Musk having a livestream with Trump on X. Ms. Vestager stated before she left that oversight of social media is more important than ever. She noted that internet companies did not seem to realise that European laws, such as the new Digital Services Act, gave European regulators greater power to curb illegal speech on social media that undermines democracy. She further noted that Mr. Musk's closeness to President Trump is in danger of influencing regulation of the former's social media company X, an issue under investigation by the European Commission.

In fact, US tech giants will most likely be very pleased when Vestager leaves as well. Therein lies the potential effectiveness of the legislation which was so effective under Breton and Vestager as legislation is only good as its enforcers. Vestager will be remembered as the chief antagonist of the tech giants as the DMA which she championed investigating the monopolistic abuse of the Big Tech gatekeepers against their perceived rivals.

The future is unknown without the two EU champions of competition law and regulation to restrain the tech giants from unfair competition practices on their digital platforms.[1,2] Yet, the number of cases against tech giants keeps rising, and the European Commission is relentless in bringing these cases, and many last for years with fines levied for unfair competition and then appeals. An example would be in 2019, the European Commission found that Google had used its dominance to block rival Internet advertisers.

Google had a victory with the EU regulators concerning Google placing restrictive terms in contracts with third-party websites which blocked rivals from placing their own adverts on those websites which is illegal. On 18 September 2024, the EU's General Court noted that restrictive clauses in contracts with third-party websites had not harmed consumers nor deterred innovation. Neither was there evidence that the clauses supported Google in maintaining a dominant position on the markets for online search advertising. Google also noted that in 2016 before the European Commission had decided to impose a €1.5 billion competition fine, it had amended its contracts. This win against the EU antitrust fine appeal was a victory for Google and indicated that cases against tech giants in relation to unfair competition can be handled fairly.[3]

Nobel Prize Winners

When tech giants such as Google claim that they are working for the greater good and only they hold the power and financial clout to turn into reality big ideas that involve greater abilities to communicate, for example, it is difficult to dismiss this when they have trained AI scientists who recently won the Nobel Prize for Chemistry.

Demis Hassabis, the chief executive of Google's primary artificial intelligence lab, and John Jumper, one of the lab's scientists, were two of the three of researchers who received the Nobel Prize in Chemistry for their efforts to better understand the human body and fight disease through AI.[4] The day before, a former Vice President of Google, Geoffrey Hinton, won the Nobel Prize for Physics again in the AI field.

AI is increasingly becoming a central interest of tech giants and has the potential to serve the needs of humankind, but as argued in my last book[5] it has the potential, if commercially and not regulated, to do great damage. Therefore, it is probably beneficial that regulators rein in the power and anti-competitive behaviour of Big Tech before it dominates AI applications through its digital platforms or uses AI to give it preferential treatment to exclude competitors. This could happen with incursions into the healthcare sector.

Algorithms Need Regulating?

Where it was once nation states that controlled speech and social communication in a country, in the digital age it is known as the algorithmic society.

Facebook is one of the founders of recommendation algorithms and the largest with 3 billion followers. This means that rather than seeing posts in chronological order which used to be the case, in the digital age Facebook lets users see what it wants them to see. As contentious posts are rewarded by algorithms, these may become overrepresented with the majority views not being given the exposure in proportion to their size. Therefore, a marketplace of ideas in which everyone is heard equally will not occur with social media.[6]

Professors Kai Riemer and Sandra Peter of the University of Sydney Business School note that by determining the audience for each piece of content that's posted, platforms "sever the direct relationship between speakers and their audiences", and "Speech is no longer organised by speaker and audience, but by algorithms." It's something that they claim is not acknowledged in the current debates over free speech – which focuses on "the speaking side of speech". And, they argue, it "interferes with free speech in unprecedented ways".[7]

Therefore, another area of tech giants' dominance in social communication through social media also needs to be regulated by an independent judicial body and regulator before free speech and content is compromised.

Promotion of Nuclear Power to Maintain Data Centres

Tech giants are using vast amounts of energy to maintain their data centres for AI needs.

Google for example, is initiating the building of new digital age small nuclear reactors, which they claim are climate friendly clean energy and can assist with providing AI for everyone. Google has created plans with Kairos Power based in California to build a demonstration nuclear reactor in Tennessee which began construction in July 2024. In 2023, US Regulators gave Kairos Power the first permit in 50 years to build a new type of nuclear reactor. In March 2024 Amazon stated that it would buy a nuclear-powered data centre in Pennsylvania.

In this case, the US Nuclear Regulatory Commission, in addition to local agencies, will have input into where these nuclear reactors are sited.[7] Regulatory agencies are in place to guard against abuses of potentially dangerous energy sources. This is in contradistinction to Competition Law regulators, which have only just recently become keenly aware of the need to modernise their efforts to deal with unfair competition on digital platforms.

Democracy and Free Speech for Humans Is in Peril?

The central point of the analysis in this book assesses the urgent requirement for Competition Law globally and specifically in Japan, China, the UK, EU, and the USA to modernise mirroring the rapid growth of digital technology. One of the main manifestations of unfair competition globally organised by Big Tech companies for their benefit and profit is using their digital platforms to be self-preferential in their online marketplace and control of information and content.

The implications of this unfair competition are monumental, as all the struggles and conflicts of the 21st century are dwarfed by the ferocity for control of populations by Big Tech companies and national governments. This is occurring to the point that whole political systems such as Democracy are at stake, with authoritarian states increasing. AI which as noted in my last book, can have very positive effects on humanity, as well as dangerous ones such as reshaping the nature of speech communication and information is part of the power struggle for control over free speech and as intellectual Yuval Noah Harari noted in his latest book *Nexus*, free speech is vital and for humans rather than algorithms from Big Tech companies to decide. In the final analysis, it is humans for geopolitical reasons who are deciding to follow new Competition Law regulations or not, depending on political considerations. In the US many Republicans under President Trump's lead vigorously defended Meta for eliminating its fact checking programme and scaling back its content restrictions before Trump's inauguration. Others, such as Senator Marsha Blackburn (R-Tennessee), views it as a cynical move to avoid regulation, while outgoing FTC Chair Lina Khan suggested it was a decision made to gain leverage in the forthcoming lawsuits against Meta to be pursued by incoming regulators. Therefore, the other tech giants discussed in this book may follow the Meta lead.[8]

Notes

1 Cristiano Lima-Strong, 'The E.U. Is Losing Two Titans of Tech Regulation, Testing Its Resolve', Tech Brief, *The Washington Post*, 17, September 2024.
2 Adam Sartariano, 'The World's Pioneering Tech Cop Is Making Her Exit', *New York Times*, 26 November 2024.
3 Louisa Clarence-Smith, 'Google Wins EU Antitrust Fine Appeal', *The Times*, 19 September 2024.
4 Cade Metz, Steve Lohr, David McCabe, 'Google Triumphs on the Nobel Stage as Tough Antitrust Fight Looms', *New York Times,* 9 October 2024.
5 Ruth Taplin, *Artificial Intelligence Intellectual Property, Cyber Risk and Robotics; A New Digital Age,* 'Conclusion', (Abingdon; Routledge, 2023).
6 Nicholas Barret, 'How Have Social Media Algorithms Changed the Way We Interact?' *BBC Online,* 13 October 2024.
7 Joao de Silva, 'Google Turns to Nuclear to Power AI Data Centres', *BBC Online,* 15 October 2024.
8 Cristiano Lima Strong, 'Meta Is Wooing the GOP. These Republicans Aren't Buying It', Tech Brief, *The Washington Post*, 15 January 2025.

Index

Bold page numbers indicate tables.

D

Made in the USA
Monee, IL
31 July 2026

9347afe0-2282-43ce-bb90-8b90863515fcR01